Naomi Honda

Success factors needed in high quality software development

Naomi Honda

Success factors needed in high quality software development

Practice of Software quality accounting

LAP LAMBERT Academic Publishing

Cover image: www.ingimage.com

Publisher:
LAP LAMBERT Academic Publishing
is a trademark of
Dodo Books Indian Ocean Ltd. and OmniScriptum S.R.L publishing group

120 High Road, East Finchley, London, N2 9ED, United Kingdom
Str. Armeneasca 28/1, office 1, Chisinau MD-2012, Republic of Moldova, Europe
Managing Directors: Ieva Konstantinova, Victoria Ursu
info@omniscriptum.com

ISBN: 978-3-8484-1037-8

Zugl. / Approved by: Tottori, University of Tottori, 2013

Research on success factors neded

in achieving high quality software development

-Construction, practice and significance

of software quality accounting-

Naomi Honda

Table of Contents

4

Chapter 1. Introduction

1.1 Background

The term "software crisis" used to mean the gap between supply and demand of software production during the 1970's. In all probability, now in the modern era, we are on the verge of a second software crisis. As we look around our society, we can see that software is used in the vast majority of products, such as television sets, refrigerators and other home appliances. Also, the reliability of public systems that support the social foundation such as trains, airplanes, and banks is underpinned by software. To implement functionalities that we find convenient or attractive, software is now a common choice. Without software our society could not be maintained as it is today. However, can we be sure that manufacturers are providing software that guarantees the quality that they should provide or that we expect them to provide?

The term "software" first came into the world in 1958. The concept of "software engineering" was first introduced 10 years later, in 1968. The first appearance of the term "software" in Japan was allegedly in an article of the newspaper, Asahi Shimbun [1-1]. So now in 2013, it is 55 years since the birth of software, 45 years since the onset of software engineering, and only 44 years since the term "software" was first mentioned in a Japanese newspaper. In less than 50 years, software has grown remarkably widespread throughout society.

In such a short history, has the quality of software improved in proportion to the importance it bears? In many cases, the symptoms of possible failures are overlooked during the development phase, leading to a delay in time to market and resulting in problems that are uncovered after release to market. These circumstances happen time after time, resulting in a deleterious impact on economic activities. For manufacturers, the improvement of software quality is now the priority issue to solve, not only to sustain their businesses, but also to allow them to fulfill their social responsibilities.

There are two main reasons for the difficulty of ensuring software quality. The first reason is that, although software has come to spread throughout and dominate society in just about 50 years since its birth, industries have not been able to build systems to deploy high quality software in such a short period of time. Cars, for example, became affordable to consumers about 100 years after they were first manufactured. On the contrary, software has become a popular tool everywhere in society in just 50 years. Software cannot operate alone; it requires hardware to run on. Due to the surprising improvement in the hardware cost performance, software has been able to become widely and instantly accepted by a number of users. Unfortunately, the difficulties of ensuring software quality are not recognized by the general public. Instead, the public understanding is that software can be created and modified quite easily.

The second reason lies in software's unique characteristics. These characteristics are greatly different from those of hardware. That is, software is intangible, and software is a chunk of logic. No current technologies can completely address these characteristics. This seems to be impeding high quality software development to a large extent.

"The second software crisis" explains the situation where society as a whole heavily relies on software with no real guarantee of quality; however citizens are not aware of this. In other words, software is used everywhere in society, and is assuming responsibility for the systems that support the foundation of society, which depend on its reliability. Nevertheless, software vendors are struggling to guarantee quality, while the difficulty of maintaining quality is not recognized by the general public. The spread of software throughout society has progressed rapidly, while the maintenance of the technology and industry that utilizes it cannot keep up with it. In this modern society plugged into software, immediate action must be taken without wasting any more time.

1.2   Objectives

This author has been working in an organization with a long history as the first software development division established at NEC, and for over 20 years since then, has been in charge of quality assurance for software products developed by the organization. The organization currently has approximately 5000 people working as software technicians, and the author is responsible for the quality assurance of the software products developed by those 5000 people. To address the problem of too many defects [1] found after release to market, the organization devised a quality management method called "Software Quality Accounting", which has been built up and operated for over 20 years. Furthermore, to make software quality accounting function effectively, the organization has been establishing a supporting framework to facilitate quality accounting. Putting this into practice, the organization has been able to reduce and maintain the number of post-release defects to less than 5%. The author has focused on developing and applying the software quality accounting.

Coincidently, some critical elements in the fundamental philosophy of software quality accounting and its framework were also seen in those systems developed by other domestic companies for the purpose of solving software quality issues and improving their products

---

[1]   Defects: faults or errors within the software (discussed in Chapter 2)[2] The author was the leader of the survey and held the position of deputy chairperson of the SQiP Software Quality Committee that conducted the survey. The author also has experience as a leader in acquiring CMMI level 5 certification for her own organization. This was achieved in 2004.

since the 1970's. While it is true the software industry is struggling with guaranteeing software quality, there are some practices that have been proven to produce positive results.

Also, a variety of technologies have being proposed for improving software quality. CMMI (Capability Maturity Model Integration) [1-2] is the leading technology. The quality accounting design organization that the author works for achieved CMMI level 5 (highest level) at the beginning of the year 2000. The author was the leader of the CMMI achievement project. The SEI (Software Engineering Institute) in the US, that advocates CMMI, says in one of its reports that, among the organizations worldwide that try to obtain CMMI certification, only 0.6 % of them comprise over 2,000 people and have achieved the level 5.

Based on the experience and research above, this dissertation will discuss software quality accounting techniques and how to achieve positive results from quality accounting. Furthermore, while discussing the values of software quality accounting from an engineering viewpoint, the success factors for high quality software development will be discussed. Thus, this paper will illustrate the path to follow for fostering successful high quality software development technologies and systems to handle the second software crisis.

1.3   Structure of this Dissertation

This dissertation is composed of 10 chapters including this one, Chapter 1.

Chapter 2 discusses the issues that impede high quality software development. "Quality" and "Defects", which are the key words for this dissertation, are defined relative to various standards and research, and the relation between them is also clarified. These topics are baseline for discussing quality management. The chapter then continues to discuss software characteristics and their impact on the software industry. At the same time, the issues impeding high quality software development will be identified based on the results of investigation into Japan's CMMI level 5 organizations.

Chapter 3 introduces the methodology of "Software Quality Accounting" and how to apply it. The author has been working on developing and defining "Software Quality Accounting" for over 20 years. It is a solution that was devised by organizations that were bothered by a number of defects found in software after its release to market, and is expected to be key to achieving high quality software development.

Chapter 4 describes the methodological features and practical application of "defect analysis and 1+n procedure," which is one of the components of software quality accounting. The reason for individually addressing "defect analysis and 1+n policy" in this chapter, is because defect analysis is an important technique that will have a great impact on the improvement activities of an organization.

Chapter 5 discusses a review methodology as well as some of the quality assurance practices that support Software Quality Accounting. A review methodology is important in that Software Quality Accounting is a quality management technique that places importance on reviews. Also, Software Quality Accounting is not the sole producer of all positive results. A supporting framework, developed to help make efficient use of Software Quality Accounting, has been contributing to increases in quality as well. Consequently, this framework has been implemented in the same way as in other domestic companies that have been addressing issues of software quality improvement since the 1970's. Therefore, a key to achieving high quality software development could be found by exploring these commonalities.

Chapter 6 discusses a software factory as a system that integrates development methodologies, tools and development environments. This is the foundation of software quality/productivity improvement. The latest progress involving the software factory will be introduced.

Chapter 7 introduces three actual examples of quality improvements made through the application of software quality accounting. These examples are taken from those projects for which the author was the leader in promoting quality improvement activities. In every example, software quality accounting was rigorously applied, while maintaining the supporting framework to help the system.

Chapter 8, taking into account all previous chapters, discusses software quality accounting from an engineering viewpoint. Chapter 9 identifies the primary factors of success with high quality software development and an overall perspective.

Lastly, Chapter 10 concludes with a summary of this dissertation, followed by issues to address in the future.

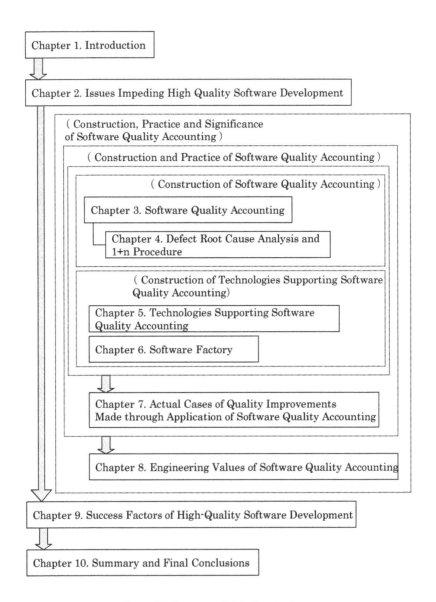

Figure 1-1 Structure of this dissertation

Chapter 2. Issues Impeding High Quality Software Development

2.1 Introduction

This chapter discusses the issues that impede high quality software development from various perspectives surrounding software development.

To begin with, the key word "quality" as well as "defect," which are critical to software development, are defined referring to various standards and research results. Then, the definition of quality management and the management targets will be discussed. In addition, software characteristics will be identified to show that the difficulty with software is rooted both, in the nature of software, and in the secondary effects resulting from that nature. Issues impeding high quality software development that are caused by software difficulties will also be explained from the perspective of the software industry. In order to bring out the issues that impede high quality software development in the field, the author makes use of the investigation results from CMMI level 5 compliant organizations to consider process capability maturity, while identifying what can or cannot be achieved by CMMI. The reason for using these investigation results is to extract the issues that impede high quality software development on the condition that no software process functionalities are missed.

2.2 What is Quality?

The term "quality" is used with many different meanings. These include usages that refer to something that can be apprehended directly, such as the occurrence of a fault, others such as attractiveness that are difficult to pin down, and also its use to indicate a clear superiority in terms of functions or other aspects of performance. Having been defined in a variety of ways by different researchers and technical standards, the term has no single agreed definition. What can be said to be generally agreed, however, is that the ultimate goal of quality is customer satisfaction. This applies not only to software, but also across the full range of products, including hardware and services.

This chapter will discuss "quality" with reference to definitions by researchers and technical standards. Table 2-1 lists a number of these definitions. The chapter will focus in particular on the differences between quality in the general sense and quality in the field of software.

Table 2-1 Different Definitions of Quality

Category	Standard/Researcher	Definition of quality	Remarks
Widely used cross-industry definition of quality	ISO9000	The degree to which a set of inherent characteristics fulfills requirement	ISO9000 defines a requirement as a "need or expectation that is stated, generally implied or obligatory".
	Joseph M. Juran	·Product features which meet the needs of customers and thereby provide satisfaction ·Free from problems (faults or mistakes)	Quality is defined based on these two aspects (see below)
	Philip B. Crosby	Fitness for purpose	
Definition of quality for software	Gerald M. Weinberg	Quality is value to some person	This expresses how "value" is different depending on different people's perspectives, such as users, system administrators, project managers (relativity of quality).
	James Martin	Meeting the true business (or user) requirements as effectively as possible at the time the system comes into operation	A feature of this definition is that it focuses on shorter development periods and responding to customer needs that change over time. It explains the need for RAD in terms of this way of thinking.
	Roger S. Pressman	Conformance to explicitly stated functional and performance requirements, explicitly documented development standards, and implicit characteristics that are expected of all professionally developed software	This expresses the idea that quality defects will almost surely result if development standards are not followed.
	ISO/IEC25000	The ability of a software product to satisfy stated and implied needs when used under specified conditions	
	IEEE Std 610	The degree to which a system, component, or process meets customer or user needs or expectations	This definition refers not only to the quality of systems and component (software products) but also to process quality.
Approach to quality in Japan	Kaoru Ishikawa	·Narrow definition of quality: Quality of product itself ·Broad definition of quality: Should consider all aspects, including the attributes of the work, service, information, affirmation, department, people, system, and companies.	Treats quality as attributes and explains it as follows in terms of narrow and broad definitions. Ishikawa saw quality management as being fundamentally about the management of this broad definition of attributes. He has had a major influence on the Japanese approach to quality management.
	Noriaki Kano	·Must-be quality: One that will be taken for granted if adequately provided, but that will result in dissatisfaction if inadequate. ·One-dimensional quality: One that will result in satisfaction if adequately provided and dissatisfaction if inadequate. ·Attractive quality: One that will result in satisfaction if adequately provided, but which will be considered acceptable even if inadequate.	This explains quality in terms of "must-be quality" and "attractive quality".
	Yoshinori Iizuka	Overall impression of applicable characteristics that relate to needs	The expression "relate to needs" indicates that quality applies to the characteristics of the needs felt by customers. It also explains quality as being something determined by the values of an external group, namely those customers.

2.2.1 Explicit and Implicit Needs

In the ISO9000 series of international standards for quality management systems (ISO9000 quality management systems — Fundamentals and vocabulary), quality is defined as the "degree to which a set of inherent characteristics fulfills requirement" [2-1]. After the definition of quality, ISO9000 also provides a definition of a "requirement" as being a "need or expectation that is stated, generally implied or obligatory". That is, the definition includes both explicit and implicit needs. Together, these two definitions indicate that quality is the degree to which both explicit and implicit needs are satisfied. Implicit needs are those that are normal or customary for the person concerned. Ease-of-use is a clear example of an implicit need. That is, along with products needing to be satisfactory in terms of function, there are also unstated but obvious requirements for them to be easy to use.

The ISO9001 standard applies to organizations that supply any type of product or service, not just software. Accordingly, taking account of implicit as well as explicit needs can be equated to generic "common sense" that applies to the supply of products and services, including such things as hardware. On the other hand, when considering the situation in practical software development, taking account of implicit needs cannot be described as something that occurs as a matter of course. To the extent that the industry is still at this stage, the identification and consideration of implicit needs are important to quality software.

2.2.2 Building in Quality at the Process Level

In "Software Engineering: A Practitioner's Approach", author Roger S. Pressman defined quality as "conformance to explicitly stated functional and performance requirements, explicitly documented development standards, and implicit characteristics that are expected of all professionally developed software" [2-2].

Of particular note is the reference to "explicitly documented development standards". Following on from this definition, Pressman writes that, "if the criteria [documented development standards] are not followed, lack of quality will almost surely result."

The same idea is expressed in the IEEE Std 610 international standard. IEEE Std 610 defines quality as the "degree to which a system, component, or process meets customer or user needs or expectations". A point to note here is that the definition includes not only systems and components, but also processes. In other words, the extent to which processes satisfy user needs has a major bearing on quality. IEEE Std 610 is a glossary of software engineering terms, meaning that this definition was made with software in mind.

As these examples show, the idea that a lack of quality will result if software development does not follow correct processes (such as development standards) is so widely accepted that it is part of the definitions used in international standards. While the attitude that, "so long as the end product works correctly, it does not matter how it is built" can sometimes be heard expressed in the software development workplace, this is a mistake. That quality is something that has to be built in at the process level is also "common sense" in software.

2.2.3   Software-Focused Definitions

The definition given by Gerald M. Weinberg is that "quality is value to some person" [2-3]. This expresses the idea that "value" is a matter of perspective. A particular software will have a number of different stakeholders, such as the person who uses it directly, their managers, the system operators, and so on. This definition means that the software's "value" is different for each person. This is called the "relativity of quality". For example, the people who use the software directly want to be able to do so intuitively without having to read a manual. Their manager in turn may value the readability of the output, whereas system operators will want software that is trouble-free. This makes it very important that the different people involved with the software are categorized, and that consideration is given to what constitutes "value" for each group.

James Martin, the person who introduced the term, "rapid application development" (RAD), defined quality as "meeting the true business (or user) requirements as effectively as possible at the time the system comes into operation" [2-4]. A feature of this definition is the strong emphasis it places on time. The rapid pace of change in the IT industry is something that needs no further explanation. It is because of this recognition of the rapid pace of change that the definition places value on being able to keep up with needs as they change over time. In simple terms, there is considerable value in the act of providing a software at a designated time. It is the timing itself that gives it value. It implies that, along with the current recognition of the challenges of achieving a high level of quality and productivity in software development, quality should also be seen in terms of being able to develop software that can satisfy specific requirements on schedule.

2.2.4   Approach to Quality in Japan

A major feature of how quality is thought of in Japan is "customer orientation". This is said to have had a major influence when seen against the Western approach of describing quality in terms of product features.

Kaoru Ishikawa, who has had a major influence on quality management in Japan, was notable for looking at product quality in terms of its attributes [2-5]. Differentiating between a narrow definition of product quality that relates only to the product itself and a broad definition that takes in all of the attributes that have an impact on the product (including the attributes of the work, department, and people, for example), he saw quality management as being fundamentally about the management of this broad concept of quality.

Noriaki Kano explained quality from the perspectives of "attractive quality", "must-be quality", and "one-dimensional quality" [2-6]. This concept of quality was explained in terms of the customer's psychological sense of satisfaction and the physical adequacy provided by the attributes of the product or service. An "attractive quality" is a characteristic that delivers a psychological sense of satisfaction if the associated physical attribute is adequately provided, but which will be considered acceptable even if inadequate. A "must-be quality" is one that will be taken for granted if the physical attribute is adequately provided, but that will result in dissatisfaction if inadequate. Similarly, a "one-dimensional quality" is one in which there is a proportional relationship between the physical attribute and the level of psychological satisfaction, such that satisfaction results if the physical attribute is adequately provided, and dissatisfaction if inadequate. A must-be quality will result in customer complaints if not fulfilled. A high level of attractive qualities can result in a popular product.

Yoshinori Iizuka defined quality as the "overall impression of applicable characteristics that relate to needs" [2-7]. The expression "relate to needs" indicates that quality applies to the characteristics of the needs felt by the customers of the product or service. It also explains quality as being something determined by the values of an external group, namely those customers. This is a very important factor to consider when thinking about quality; that it is determined not by the supplier of the product or service but by the values of its customers, who are separate from the supplier.

The "customer orientation" that is a feature of how quality is thought of in Japan is very important because the support of customers is critical to the ongoing growth of companies. The more satisfied customers purchase the products and services supplied by a company, the more the company can earn. The company can then reinvest these earnings to produce new products or services. It is through this virtuous circle that companies achieve ongoing growth. For companies to survive and maintain their strength into the future, they must continue to satisfy a wide range of customers over the long term. This means that customer orientation demands a genuinely long-term approach.

2.2.5   Definitions Based on Quality Characteristics

The ISO/IEC9126 international standard defines the characteristics of software quality as shown in Fig. 2-1 [2-8]. The two quality models are respectively for external and internal quality and for quality in use. Unlike the definitions given above, these quality models treat software analytically. The model for external and internal quality classifies it in terms of six different characteristics: functionality, reliability, usability, efficiency, maintainability, and portability. While functionality and reliability tend to predominate in software development, it is important to give similar consideration to the other quality characteristics. While usability and efficiency are not usually overlooked, their being quality characteristics that customers specifically look for, there is a tendency to undervalue maintainability and portability in new developments in particular. In the current environment, where upgrades predominate and the development of entirely new software makes up a smaller proportion, it is essential to take a long-term view of the software lifecycle and consider factors such as maintainability and portability from the initial development stage. While the benefits of maintainability and portability are difficult to perceive in the short term, they are characteristics that become increasingly valuable the longer the lifecycle of the software.

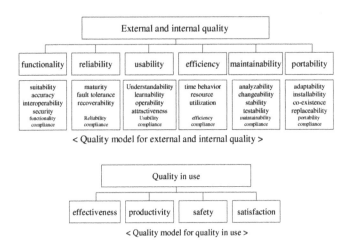

< Quality model for external and internal quality >

< Quality model for quality in use >

Fig. 2-1 Software Quality Models [ISO/IEC 9126]

2.2.6   Summary

It has been demonstrated that quality has a variety of definitions. This dissertation will adopt the ISO9000 definition of quality as being the "degree to which a set of inherent characteristics fulfills requirement". This is because, when considering quality in a corporate context, it is important to think in terms of the contradistinction between "requirements" and "characteristics that inherently should be provided". Furthermore, the term "characteristics that inherently should be provided" also implicitly suggests a distinction from the "actually implemented characteristics". Maintaining a distinction between those characteristics that inherently should be provided and those that actually are provided is very important for the companies that supply products and services. This is because the reality for software is that a gap exists between the "characteristics that inherently should be provided" and the "actually implemented characteristics". It is also necessary to remember that a "requirement" is a characteristic that applies to the customers who receive the supplied product or service. That is, requirements are judged by an external set of values that belong not to the company that supplies a product or service but to its recipient. The aim of ensuring quality, in other words, is to achieve customer satisfaction. Companies can ensure ongoing growth by achieving customer satisfaction in a way that is consistent and sustained over the long term.

Table 2-2 lists the key points for ensuring quality in the field of software. Of particular importance are to identify requirements accurately and to build in quality at the process level. Factors of importance when identifying requirements include considering implicit needs, categorizing users and considering the different needs of each group, and taking account of the six quality characteristics with reference to the software lifecycle. Of importance to building quality in at the process level are that there is value in processes that allow software to be delivered on schedule, that those processes are followed faithfully, and that they build quality into the product or service.

Table 2-2 Definition of Quality in this Dissertation and Key Points for Ensuring Software Quality

Definition of quality	Degree to which a set of inherent characteristics fulfills requirement [ISO9000 definition]
	Ultimate goal of quality is customer satisfaction
Key points for ensuring software quality	• Consider implicit as well as stated needs.
	• Faithfully follow development standards and other processes. (Quality defects will almost surely result if standards are not followed.)
	• Categorize people based on their different perspectives and consider the needs of each group.
	• Being able to deliver software on schedule itself has value.
	• Consider the six characteristics of quality: functionality, reliability, usability, efficiency, maintainability, and portability.

2.3   What is a Defect?

In software development, terms such as "bug", "problem", "fault", or "defect" are used to indicate that the software does not function as intended. This section defines what these terms mean.

2.3.1   Definition of Defect

Table 2-3 lists the definitions for defect-related terminology specified in ISO/IEC 2382-14:1997 (Information technology ·· Vocabulary ·· Reliability, maintainability and availability) [2-9]. The term "failure" is defined as indicating system shutdowns and other events that are recognizable by people, with "fault" meaning the cause of the failure. Similarly, "error" is defined as the difference between a theoretical and measured value and "defect" is used to mean a generic fault. In practice, the Japanese terms such as "kosho" (failure) and "shogai" (fault) specified in ISO/IEC 2382-14:1997 do not closely match their actual usage and have not been widely adopted. For example, the term "shogai" (fault) usually means what ISO/IEC 2382-14:1997 defines as a "kosho" (failure). Accordingly, this dissertation will use the term "defect" that is in widespread actual use to refer to what ISO/IEC 2382-14:1997 defines as a "fault". That is, the term "defect" will be used to mean an "abnormal situation in which the ability of a functional unit to perform its required function is impaired or lost" (the same as the definition for a "fault" in ISO/IEC 2382-14:1997).

Table 2-3 Definitions of Various Defect-Related Terms

Term	Definition (ISO/IEC 2382-14)	Remarks
Error	The difference between a value or status obtained by calculation, observation, or measurement and the true (specified or theoretical) value or status.	
Fault	An abnormal situation in which the ability of a functional unit to perform its required function is impaired or lost	The term "defect" is typically used in the sense of "fault". The same applies to terms such as "bug" or "problem".
Failure	The loss by a functional unit of its ability to perform its required function	An event that is referred to in Japanese as "trouble" is typically used in the sense of a "failure".

2.3.2   Definition of Defects During Development

This section will discuss defects during software development. There is a natural tendency to adopt a wider definition of "defect" during development. Rather than just those issues that result in the capabilities of a functional unit being impaired or lost, any issue that is deemed to require correction is treated as a defect and corrected. The violation of coding rules is a representative example. These violations are corrected even if they have no influence on actual program operation. This is done for reasons of software maintainability. Variations from the specifications, stipulations, standards, or other such requirements are also treated as defects. These would not necessarily lead to the capabilities of a functional unit being impaired or lost. Accordingly, issues that are deemed to require correction, even if they do not result in the capabilities of a functional unit being impaired or lost, are referred to as "anomalies" [2-10]. During the development process, the definition of defect shall include anomalies.

Personal Software Process (PSP) contains the definition, "defects are counted by the number of times the program is modified" [2-11]. This definition can be rephrased as "an instance where a modification is required is a defect". This means that, if something requires modification, there is a reason for this and it is this reason that is the "defect". Reasons for modification include cases that cause the capabilities of a functional unit to be impaired or lost, and cases in which the capabilities of a functional unit are not necessarily impaired or lost (anomalies, in other words).

Documentation defects at the design stage also require a more precise definition that takes account of actual practice. Design specification documents require the specifications to be specified to a level of granularity that suits the technical level of the developers. If their technical level is low, detailed explanations are required. That is, the specifications must be specified based on appropriate assumptions about the extent of implicit knowledge among the developers. Also, as the documentation of specifications cannot avoid using written explanations, the clarity of this expression has a major influence on understanding of the specifications. It requires written explanations that can be correctly interpreted by everyone concerned.

Table 2-4 gives example definitions for "defect" at the design and coding stages. These definitions are based on the assumption that anomalies are also included in defects.

Table 2-4 Example Definitions for "Defect" at Design and Coding Stages

	1	Expressions not conforming to standards are defects.
	2	Expressions not conforming to the specification of the previous process phase of the software development life cycle are defects.
	3	If there is high possibility of other team members misunderstanding the deliverable because of the ambiguity of expression then it is a defect. If the possibility of misunderstanding is low then it is not a defect.
Defect of design document	4	If the expression is lacking check with other groups then it is a defect.
	5	If not explicitly written as an expression then it is a defect. Description mistakes originating from typographical errors are not defects.
	6	If there is problem in the specification of the previous process phase in the software development life cycle which was used as the input for the current specification document, then it is a defect belonging to the previous process phase.
	7	If the defect originates from a defect of a specification document belonging to other groups, then it is a defect belonging to the other group.
Defect of coding	1	Codes not conforming to coding rules are defects
	2	Coding mistakes are defects.
Remarks		Defects with the same cause are counted together as a single instance.

2.3.3   Relationship between Process Model and Defects

Table 2-4 contains a list of example defect definitions that implicitly assumes the waterfall model. The definition of defects during development should consider the relationship with the process model. This is because it is necessary to decide the timing at which an issue is judged to be a defect. At the design and specification stage, for example, the developer performs the design and expresses it in the design specification document. This section will discuss the timing at which something is judged to be a defect.

Fig. 2-2 shows the development process assumed in Table 2-4. This is the V model. The V model is a type of waterfall model that clearly expresses the interrelationships between design and testing by visually representing the corresponding design and testing alongside each other [2-12]. That is, the V model provides a clear indication of the stage at which design work is tested by clearly representing the correspondences between design and testing.

A point to note about the V model in Fig. 2-2 is that, for each process in the design and coding stages, the design (or coding in the coding process) and review are always defined as sub-processes. The assumption is that the design specifications drawn up in a particular design process will always be reviewed in the review process for that design process. Defects in design specification documents, as referred to in Table 2-4, are defined as defects if recognized as such after the design process has completed and the review commenced.

The idea behind this definition is that defects are identified after the design is complete. A factor to be considered with this approach is at what point is the design to be deemed complete. This is something that needs to be determined based on the development process being used.

Things like the specific definition of a defect during development or the timing at which something is judged to be a defect are best defined by each of the software development organizations taking account of their respective circumstances. Making a specific definition of "defect" involves having detailed definitions of things like the development process, how the design specification is to be documented, and coding rules. Arriving at specific definitions for these at a level that can be used in practice is difficult for all but well-established organizations. As few such organizations exist, most organizations experience difficulties when defining what a defect is. This can be seen as one of the challenges facing the software industry that results from the shortness of its history.

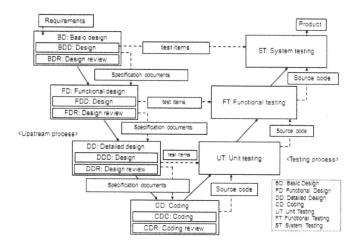

Fig. 2-2 Development Process Assumed in this Dissertation (V Model)

2.3.4 Post-Release Defects

This section will discuss defects after the software is released. The first step is to define what is meant by release. An appreciation of what is meant by release is comparatively easy in cases such as package or embedded software where a formal release date is specified, after which customers can purchase the product. However, determining release can be difficult in cases where a contract is entered into with a customer for the development of software specifically for that customer. The reason is that release can take on many different forms, such as when system testing is conducted jointly with the customer, or when the customer is provided with unfinished versions of the software as a preview to assist their preparations. The only way to deal with such circumstances is to define release on a case-by-case basis. One method is to use a "release decision-making meeting" hosted by the development organization as a milestone for demarcating the pre- and post-release phases. This method can be used to judge when release has occurred regardless of the type of software.

Post-release defects can also be classified based on where the defect occurred (see Fig. 2-3). Defects can be grouped into those experienced by the customer and those found by the development organization. While defects experienced by the customer do not include anomalies, defects found by the development organization after release may include anomalies. Possible situations in which the development organization may find a defect after release include when making enhancements to the software or when it is necessary to respond to defects in the software experienced by the customer. In particular, there are cases when

21

anomalies or other problems are fixed when making enhancements to the software, including either as part of the current enhancements or to aid future enhancements.

The number of defects during development (I in Fig. 2-3) tend to increase in proportion to the size of the software development. The number of defects experienced by the customer (III), in contrast, is not proportional to the size of the software development. Rather, it is more often influenced by factors such as how customers use the software, or the number of customers in the case of a commercially available product. For example, defects are more likely to be experienced by customers in environments where a variety of different abnormal situations can arise easily, such as on systems where the software is operated at close to its performance limits. In the case of defects found by the development organization after release (II), while it might be thought that factors such as the number of customers and whether further enhancements are planned would often be influential, because circumstances tend to be different in each case, no trends are evident.

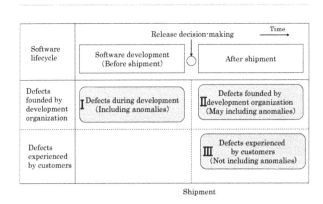

Fig. 2-3 Software Lifecycle and Defects

Fig. 2-4 shows scatter plots of the relationship between development size and defects during development (I), and between development size and defects experienced by the customer (III). While the horizontal axes representing development size have the same scale on both graphs, different scales are used for the vertical axes because the numbers of defects found before and after release differ widely. The coefficient of correlation between development size and defects during development (I) is 0.887, indicating a clear correlation. In contrast, the coefficient correlation of 0.149 between development size and defects experienced by the customer (III) indicates that these are not correlated.

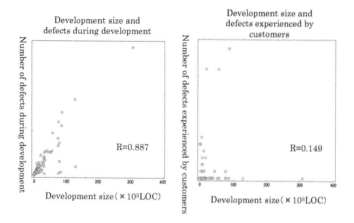

Fig. 2-4 Relationship between Development Size and Defects During Development (I) and Defects Experienced by Customer (III)

2.3.5 Relationship between Quality and Defects

This section will discuss the relationship between quality and defects.

Section 2.2 defined quality as the "degree to which a set of inherent characteristics fulfills requirement". The key elements in this definition are the "requirements", the "characteristics that inherently should be provided", and the "actually implemented characteristics". For software, a "requirement" can be thought of a characteristic perceived by the customer (recipient) of the supplied product or service, the "characteristics that inherently should be provided" as the characteristics designed by the developer, and the "actually implemented characteristics" as the characteristics actually provided by the software.

A defect, meanwhile, is defined as an "abnormal situation in which the ability of a functional unit to perform its required function is impaired or lost". While in a narrow sense the "required functions" in this definition mean the "characteristics that inherently should be provided" and that were designed by the developer, they should also include the "requirements" perceived by the customer. In contrast, what the customer sees is the "actually implemented characteristics".

In Fig. 2-5, quality is the extent to which the "characteristics that inherently should be provided" match the "requirements". Any instance where the "actually implemented characteristics" do not match the "characteristics that inherently should be provided" clearly constitutes a defect. In which case, should any mismatch between the "requirements" and the "characteristics that inherently should be provided" also be treated as a defect? The

23

"requirements" perceived by the customer can be expected to include defects. That is, the meaning of defect is not just an instance in which the product does not operate in accordance with the design; it also includes cases where characteristics that should be included are in fact not provided. For example, a design that does not satisfy important use cases in the operating environment envisaged for the software should be treated as defective because inherently necessary functions are missing. Similarly, depending on the extent, difficult-to-use designs should also be deemed defective due to their failure to satisfy an implicit need.

On the other hand, a case in which a "characteristic that inherently should be provided" exceeds the "requirement" by a significant margin is an example of "attractive quality". This is the sort of thing that can lead to something becoming a "hit product".

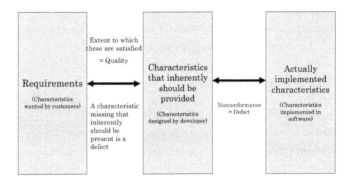

Fig. 2-5 Relationship between Quality and Defects

2.3.6   Summary

This section has discussed defects from a range of perspectives. It has considered the definition of a defect, defects during development, the relationship between the development process and defects, and the relationship between timing (whether it is before or after release) and defects. It has also discussed the relationship between quality and defects. The definition of defect used in this dissertation is an "abnormal situation in which the ability of a functional unit to perform its required function is impaired or lost", where "required function" is interpreted as meaning a "required function that inherently should be present". This meaning is somewhat broader than the normal scope of the term "defect" and indicates that the scope of the term is defined in a way that includes characteristics that inherently should be present.

Furthermore, in subsequent discussion, this dissertation will narrow down the meaning of "quality" to be "how few defects are present in software after release". This is because succeeding in developing software with few post-release defects is not only fundamental to the software industry, the increased importance of software in the modern world means that it is also a social responsibility for suppliers. It is the development of software with few post-release defects that provides the foundation for the pursuit of attractive quality that is a competitive strength.

2.4　What is Quality Management?

2.4.1　Definition of Quality Management

ISO9000 defines quality management as "a set of co-ordinated activities to direct and control an organization in order to continually improve the effectiveness and efficiency of its performance" [2-1]. Section 2.2 stated that a company's stability and survival into the future requires that it continues to satisfy a wide range of customers over the long term. Quality management means managing the company to "satisfy a wide range of customers over the long term".

While quality, cost, and delivery (QCD) have been given as the three elements of management, the "quality" element of QCD refers to quality in a very narrow sense. In contrast, the "quality" in "quality management" is an extremely broad concept that also encompasses cost and delivery. Section 2.2 also noted that the level of quality is judged by external standards, namely the criteria of the recipients of the product or service. Put another way, this implies that all activities, including quality management, should be directed toward this objective of conforming to external standards [2-7]. In this sense also, quality should be interpreted as an extremely broad concept that also encompasses cost and delivery.

2.4.2　What does Quality Management Manage?

Quality management is said to be about the management of two different areas. One approach focuses on outcomes, the other on processes [2-12]. The outcome-focused approach is about preventing defective products from leaving the company by checking that process outputs satisfy the standard. The typical method used for this purpose is inspection. Here, inspection means using some method to assess whether the result of a test or measurement passes a predefined criterion [2-12]. In the case of software development, this outcome-focused approach is applied to the outputs of each process (design specification documents, test specifications, and so on). The advantage of inspection is that it can reliably exclude non-conforming products. Unfortunately, if the number of non-conforming products is large, this can put pressure on revenue.

The process-focused approach emphasizes processes and is based on establishing processes that will produce software that is of high quality from the beginning. This approach emphasizes the establishment of processes that will produce quality products without rework, and it is based on producing products in accordance with the established processes. Accordingly, it is important to check that production always takes place in accordance with the processes. Quality management methods that place an emphasis on processes can increase the proportion of prime products. Unfortunately, reducing non-conforming products to zero is difficult. However low the proportion of non-conforming products becomes, the potential for them to be produced cannot be eliminated.

Quality assurance performed using the outcome-focused approach is called "product quality", and that performed using the process-focused approach is called "process quality". Product quality and process quality are interrelated and conducting management in a way that combines the two is considered important [2-12]. Both have advantages and disadvantages. It is important to combine them successfully and perform quality management in ways that strike a balance between the two types of quality.

2.4.3   Differences in Perspectives of Organizations and Projects

Software development typically adopts a project-based approach. A project is defined as a "time-limited activity aimed at producing a new product or service" [2-13]. Note the use of the terms "new" and "time-limited". Software development typically involves the creation of a new one-off product. Mass production is limited to the making of copies of the software. As most software development adopts a project-based approach, it is time-limited. Developers are brought together to develop new software, and the project is then disbanded once the development is complete. The project is established within an organization and its activities continue until the project ends. From the perspective of the organization, a number of internal projects are always in progress, following a cycle of formation and completion.

Management at the level of the organization has a different perspective to that at the level of the project. The objective of project-level management is to achieve the QCD goals of the project. Because each project is intended to produce a different software product, its focus should be on developing that software and achieving its QCD goals. The objective of organization-level management, in contrast, is to improve the probability that the projects being undertaken by the organization will achieve their QCD goals. To this end, in addition to analyzing the characteristics of the software development being undertaken by the organization, organization-level management also focuses on improving the probability of project success by analyzing the characteristics of successful and unsuccessful projects to establish and maintain repeatable software processes. In the case when software processes are provided by the organization, project-level management uses these processes, with the key to success being to apply them in practice while also tailoring them based on an analysis of the characteristics of the specific project.

Accordingly, it is necessary to keep in mind that the objectives and activities of management are different depending on whether that management is targeted at the organization or at a particular project.

2.5   Characteristics of Software

When considering the difficulties of software, Frederick P. Brooks, Jr. makes a distinction between those that are essential and those that are accidental [2-14]. Essential difficulties are inherent properties of software. Accidental difficulties, on the other hand, are secondary properties that emerge as a result of the inherent characteristics of software, and which are associated with the particular development but not present as a matter of course. As the intended meaning of the term "accidental difficulties" may be unclear to readers, this dissertation will use the term "secondary difficulties" in its place.

Brooks describes the essential difficulty of software as being the "specification, design, and testing of the conceptual constructs that make up an abstract software entity" [2-14]. This involves defining the customer requirements, designing the functions that the software needs to perform, designing the implementation, and confirming the validity of the result. Put another way, the hard part of software is establishing the concept and then verifying that it is correct. In contrast, secondary difficulties are those that arise primarily in the process of implementing the software. This means expressing a design in the form of a cumbersome programming language and getting it to work within the constraints of the hardware. This requires meticulousness and accuracy, and does not permit even a single mistake. There are also numerous support activities that go on around software development, with things like configuration management, the backing up of ongoing work, and the provision of development and test environments also being included among the secondary difficulties. These support activities, too, demand meticulousness and accuracy.

An essential difficulty of software is that it is very difficult to get to grips with. This is because it equates to the creation of a concept. Secondary difficulties, on the other hand, while they may be problematic, belong to the category of soluble problems. Looking at the history of software, almost all attempts at dealing with the difficulties of software have been targeted at resolving the secondary difficulties [2-14]. High-level programming languages and other development aid tools are a good example. Accordingly, it is advisable to seek comprehensive solutions to the secondary difficulties. Essential difficulties, however, are strongly affected by the inherent characteristics of software. The following sections look at the characteristics of software with reference to its relationship with its essential difficulties.

27

(1) Software is complex

Software is a collection of logical rules. It therefore grows exponentially in complexity the larger it becomes. Frederick P. Brooks, Jr. described this by saying, "A scaling-up of a software entity is not merely the repetition of the same element in larger sizes, it is necessarily an increase in the number of different elements. In most cases, the elements interact with each other in some nonlinear fashion, and the complexity of the whole increases much more than linearly."

Nevertheless, because the problems that software deals with apply to social systems and human customs and other behaviors, there is a tendency toward software becoming complex. The interfaces through which software is used are not only strongly influenced by human customs and other behaviors, they also change over time. A good example of this is the rapid transition that has occurred in computer operation from command-based to screen-based interfaces. The same applies to social systems. Commercial transactions that were once conducted face-to-face or by telephone or fax have, over a short period of time, shifted to network transactions. Despite this, there are subtle differences between industries, companies, and divisions in how these commercial transactions are conducted.

Hardware is subject to spatial constraints and other physical and scientific laws that must always be considered. Software, in contrast, faces few such constraints. What it does need to consider, however, are social systems and human customs and other behaviors that are always changing. To deal with this problem, software is forced to resort to large-scale developments. Because of the misconception that software is easy to modify, it is software that is forced to cope with last-minute modifications that cannot be dealt with by hardware. This leads to immeasurable increases in its complexity.

A result of this characteristic of software being complex is that the characteristics described in (2) and (3) below further impact on the difficulties of software.

(2) Software is not something you can see

Hardware is something you can see, touch, and feel for yourself. Products like televisions, cars, and refrigerators can also all be seen and touched. In the case of software, however, this is not possible.

The inherent complexity of software makes the tangible representation of software structures very difficult. It cannot be shown in a single diagram and instead must be expressed using a variety of diagrams with different purposes, such as showing the flow of control, flow of data, dependencies, or time-sequence of computation. As the size of software increases, even representing software by a collection of diagrams becomes impractical. It has become rare in recent years for large software projects to be developed all at once. Instead, the work is typically done as a series of separate developments. As time goes by, design policies undergo subtle changes, specifications are modified, and numerous distortions enter into the structure of the software itself. These add further to the difficulties of providing a tangible representation of software.

This characteristic of being intangible is an inherent property of software. However, it is not something that cannot be overcome. Through measures such as improving the way the design specification document is written or standardizing the diagrams to include and how information should be expressed, even software that is still under design should to some extent be able to be made tangible. Recent developments, such as the world-wide adoption of unified modeling language (UML) as a standard method for documenting designs and the availability of support tools for this purpose, indicate that, while difficult, the standardization of design specification documentation is no longer impossible. Design standardization makes it possible to quantify factors such as the size and characteristics of designs. Quantifying software development work (which is not something you can see) so that it can be understood in quantitative terms is the first step in making software tangible.

(3) Software is produced through the intellectual efforts of people

The influence of human factors in software development is immeasurable. The essential difficulty of software, that it involves creating a concept and verifying that it is correct, is something that can only be achieved through the intellectual efforts of people. Performing this sort of intellectual work under time constraints is something of which only a small number of highly talented engineers are capable. This is also something that can be seen as arising from the essential difficulties of software.

Factors such as time constraints or the expected size of the software to be developed mean that software development must be done not by an individual but by a team made up of a number of people. If there are problems with human factors, namely leadership, teamwork, communication, and the motivation that results from these, then it inevitably influences the developed software [2-15]. Engineers who do not trust their leaders will avoid talking to them, for example. This can result in their going ahead and writing software without first obtaining the information they need from the leader. The consequences of this are obvious. While hardware design is also performed through the intellectual efforts of people, the definitive difference is in the number of people involved. The number of people required for software development is typically an order of magnitude larger than for hardware design. The difficulty of communication is said to increase exponentially as the number of people increases, and communication problems pose a significant challenge to the field of software development where projects can involve large numbers of people.

On the subject of the problems posed by human factors, Frederick P. Brooks, Jr wrote, "To be successful, the quality of the people involved in a project, the form of their organization, and their management are significantly more important factors than the tools they use or the technical approaches they adopt" [2-14]. While the fact that human factors influence software development is an essential characteristic of software, there are ways of overcoming the problem. For as long as humans have existed, human factors have always posed problems in all areas of activity and our history has been one of continually overcoming the challenges of this problem domain. Measures for dealing with this include appointing appropriate people to each key role and establishing an organization in which management always includes the human factors, creating a culture in which developers have mutual respect and take pride in producing high-quality software, adopting supportive practices that can comprehensively resolve the secondary difficulties of software, and establishing software processes that concentrate on overcoming the essential difficulties. Measures like these should not only go a long way toward resolving problems that are closely entwined with human factors; they should also open up the potential for software development that can make the impossible possible.

2.6   Issues Raised by Survey of CMMI Level 5 Organization

This section discusses the challenges in the way of achieving high-quality software development based on the results of a survey[2] of Japanese organizations that had achieved CMMI level 5 in Japan. Capability Maturity Model Integration (CMMI) was developed by the Software Engineering Institute (SEI) of Carnegie Mellon University [1-2]. It divides the capability maturity of software processes into five levels and stipulates the requirements that must be met at each level. As achieving level 5 certification requires an appraisal by qualified auditors, it can provide objective proof that a company's software processes have a certain level of capability. As a software process improvement tool, CMMI has become recognized as a de facto standard.

2.6.1 Survey Summary

The following is a summary of the survey:
- Survey objective:
  By questioning organizations that have achieved mature process capabilities, identify what is significant about process capability maturity and the factors that are obstructive or beneficial to its achievement, and clarify what the concept means.
- Survey questions: Motivations for achieving level 5, consequences of achievement, and lessons learned
- Organizations surveyed: Japanese organizations that had achieved CMMI level 5
- Responses: Responses were received from 12 organizations (the total number of Japanese organizations that had achieved CMMI level 5 at the time of the survey was about 20)
- Date of survey: July 2009
- Conducted by: SQiP Software Quality Committee, Union of Japanese Scientists and Engineers

2.6.2 Summary of Survey Results

Figs. 2-6 to 2-12 and Tables 2-5 to 2-9 give a summary of the survey results. Note that some survey questions permitted multiple answers.

Seven organizations (more than half) listed "establish quantitative management" as one of the advantages of seeking CMMI certification (see Table 2-6). Eight organizations (more than half) listed "tendency for processes to become formalized" as one of the disadvantages. Processes becoming formalized were used in the sense of "unnecessary work or an increase in unnecessary process areas, etc.". In response to the question on whether respondents would recommend CMMI to other organizations, a surprising 40% said "no" (see Fig. 2-10). The reasons for this included "benefits do not justify cost" and "achieving the level tends to become the goal in itself" (see Table 2-7). Of the 60% who said they would recommend CMMI, the most common reason, given by four organizations, was "because it enables systematic process improvement". However, two organizations commented that they would recommend CMMI "not for the purpose of achieving the level, but only if genuine improvement could be achieved", indicating that while CMMI might have certain benefits, some caution is required in practice to prevent achieving the level from becoming an end in itself.

In response to the question about whether mature process capabilities led to improved quality, eleven organizations (all except one) responded that it did, indicating that process maturity has certain benefits for quality (see Fig. 2-11). The one dissenting organization responded that "while process maturity reduced variation in quality, it had little relationship with process improvement". When questioned about the number of post-release defects, half of the respondents replied that they were equivalent to or better than the average for Japan (0.020 defects/KLOC), and that when worse than the average for Japan they were equivalent to or better than the level for India (0.263 defects/KLOC) (see Fig. 2-12). These figures for post-release defects are based on material published in 2003 in the IEEE Software Magazine [2-16].

Regarding the essential factors for improving quality, the highest score went to "human factors" such as an emphasis on quality in the attitudes of team members and organizational culture, which was indicated by five respondents (see Table 2-8). The next highest were, in order, quantification, leadership of senior management, and reviews. The question on which technologies and know-how aid quality improvement drew a variety of responses, including management technologies, development technologies, review technologies, and testing technologies (see Table 2-9). Technologies supported by more than one organization included "methods for project estimation" and "review and inspection", each of which was indicated by three respondents. A point to note here is that many of the technologies have been familiar for some time. Of the 18 types of technology and know-how, the two that have only emerged comparatively recently were "extreme derivative development process (XDDP)" and "test first".

31

2.6.3   What is Process Capability Maturity?

Two key terms frequently mentioned when considering the advantages and other benefits of process capability maturity and its essential factors are "quantification and visualization" and "human factors". In contrast, an issue that comes up often when considering the disadvantages and other problems is that of "processes becoming formalized".

"Quantification and visualization" and "human factors" relate to the essential difficulties of software. Quantification and Visualization are ways of getting around the fact that software is not something you can see. Human factors, in turn, relate to the fact that software is developed through the intellectual efforts of people. The survey showed that the respondent organizations saw the greatest merit in measures and outcomes that confronted the difficulties of software directly. In contrast, given that "processes becoming formalized" means an increase in unnecessary work or unnecessary process areas, this indicates that they do not deliver any practical benefit. This in turn indicates that process capability maturity is about delivering practical benefits through measures that confront the difficulties of software directly.

An obstacle to process capability maturity is the difficulty of delivering practical benefits. The problem of "processes becoming formalized" means there is an awareness among the people involved that it can frequently lead to unnecessary processes that do not produce any practical benefits. Quantification is something that all software development organizations do. That the number one advantage of achieving level 5 (identified by a majority of respondents) was quantitative management is indicative of the difficulty of achieving practical benefits.

A beneficial aspect of process capability maturity is the correct use of familiar technologies, with quantitative management and reviews in particular offering potential benefits. The key ideas of "improvement consciousness" and "emphasis on quality in the attitudes of team members" that can be taken from the survey indicate that measures aimed at encouraging change in the attitudes of developers are also important.

2.6.4 What CMMI Can Resolve, and What it Cannot

The survey results indicate that adopting CMMI can be expected to deliver some improvement in quality. In terms of the number of post-release defects, half of the respondents ranked themselves either equivalent to India or otherwise worse than the average for Japan. Being ranked equivalent to India means that, for a software system with a size of 100 KLOC (1 KLOC = 10^3 LOC), 26 defects will be detected by the customer in the first year after release. In the author's experience, this level of defects will likely result in customer dissatisfaction in the Japanese market. This indicates how difficult it is, even with CMMI level 5, to achieve a level of quality that makes a low number of post-release defects into a competitive strength.

The implementation of quantitative management, given as one of the advantages of seeking CMMI certification, is an important process area for CMMI. It is also an area in which the adoption of CMMI can be expected to deliver benefits. Although it is not directly evident in the survey responses, the underlying objective of CMMI is the establishment of processes that are not missing anything in terms of functions, and this is one of its major advantages. The achievement of level 5 certifies that the organization has implemented all 22 process areas defined in CMMI. As many problems that arise during development are the result of functional inadequacies in the processes themselves, they can be prevented preemptively. Meanwhile, respondents identified processes becoming formalized as a disadvantage, and this can be seen as indicating that not all process areas are necessarily effective. While CMMI was meant to be a tool for achieving the objectives of users, these sorts of problem often arise when the objective shifts to being the achievement of the level itself.

The human factor of an emphasis on quality in the attitudes of team members and organizational culture was identified as an essential factor for quality improvement. The human factor is a problem associated with how an organization approaches what it is doing; it is not identified as one of the process areas in CMMI. This means that the human factor is not directly related to work on CMMI.

Based on this, the issues that CMMI should be capable of resolving are reducing the number of post-release defects by a certain extent, the establishment of comprehensive processes that are not missing anything in terms of functions, and the implementation of quantitative management. On the other hand, objectives that are difficult to achieve through the adoption of CMMI are reducing the number of post-release defects sufficiently to make it a competitive strength, establishing effective processes, and improving human factors. For these objectives that are difficult to achieve through CMMI, no definitive technological solutions are available.

2.7   Conclusion

Companies ensure their ongoing growth by achieving customer satisfaction in a way that is consistent and sustained over the long term. The objective of quality is customer satisfaction. An important feature of quality is that it is judged by external standards, namely the needs of customers. In this sense, quality is not the narrow meaning of Q as used in the term QCD (the three elements of management: quality, cost, and delivery) but should be interpreted as a broad concept that also includes C and D. Key points for ensuing quality in software are an accurate understanding of the requirements and the practice of building in quality at the process level.

"Defect" is an important quality-related term in software development. When quality is given its broad meaning, "defect" should be interpreted not in the narrow sense of something that does not operate in accordance with the design, but also as including situations in which a characteristic that inherently should be present has not been implemented.

The difficulties of software consist of essential difficulties that arise from the inherent characteristics of software, and secondary difficulties that arise in the practical production of software. The essential difficulties of software are establishing the concept and then verifying that it is correct. The secondary difficulties are the large amounts of work that require meticulousness and accuracy. These occur in areas that relate primarily to the implementation of software. The essential difficulties arise from the inherent characteristics of software, namely its complexity, its intangibility, and the fact that it is produced through the intellectual efforts of people. It cannot be said that the software industry correctly understands these characteristics of software, and this is why the industry is described as a labor-intensive one.

In addition to adopting rigorous measures for taming the secondary difficulties of software, the development of high-quality software demands a dual approach that also includes adopting strategic measures for dealing with the inherent characteristics of software. A critical factor in this approach is that it leads to measures that deliver practical results, as opposed to being formalities. Management technologies (especially quantitative management and management of human factors) and reviews are among the key concepts associated with the technologies and know-how that are effective at delivering benefits, and an important factor in this is to achieve benefits by making correct use of existing technologies. Amongst these, the issues that CMMI is able to resolve are the establishment of comprehensive processes that are not missing anything in terms of functions, reducing the number of post-release defects by a certain extent, and the implementation of quantitative management. The issues that are difficult to resolve using CMMI are reducing the number of post-release defects sufficient to make it a competitive strength, establishing effective processes, and improving human factors. The following chapters of this dissertation will discuss how these can be achieved and the issues they raise.

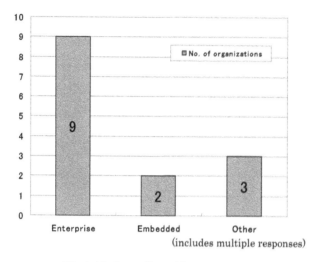

(includes multiple responses)

Fig. 2-6 Industry Type of Survey Participants
— Results of survey of organizations with CMMI level 5 (1) —

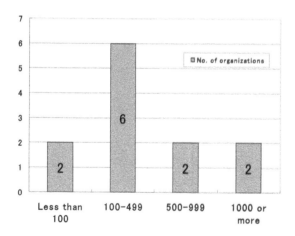

Fig. 2-7 Number of Employees of Survey Participants
— Results of survey of organizations with CMMI level 5 (1) —

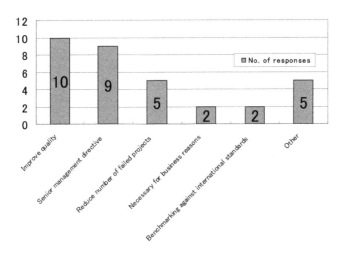

Fig. 2-8 Objective of Seeking CMMI Level 5
ー Results of survey of organizations with CMMI level 5 (2) ー

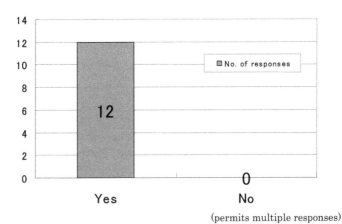

(permits multiple responses)

Fig. 2-9 Did Achievement of Level 5 Resolve Issues?
ー Results of survey of organizations with CMMI level 5 (2) ー

Table 2-5 Issues that were Resolved

─ Results of survey of organizations with CMMI level 5 (3) ─

№	Specific details of resolution
1	Significant reduction in number of failed projects (3)
2	Quality improvement (2): - 77% reduction in post-release defects over 3 years - 50% reduction in post-release defects over 4 years
3	Productivity improvement (2): - 17% reduction in testing costs - 44% improvement in web development productivity over 4 years
4	Identify strengths and weaknesses (2):
5	Make organization more attractive
6	Improve awareness among team members
7	Establish management practices, quantitative management, establish improvement cycle

Note: Issue of projects with insufficient follow-up not resolved

(Figures in brackets indicate number of organizations that gave response)

Table 2-6 Advantages and Disadvantages of Seeking CMMI

─ Results of survey of organizations with CMMI level 5 (3) ─

№	Advantages of seeking CMMI
1	Establish quantitative management (7)
2	Establish improvement consciousness (3)
3	Identify weaknesses (2)
4	Awareness of importance of step-by-step improvement
5	Self-confidence of achieving level 5
6	Raise level of quality

№	Disadvantages of seeking CMMI
1	Tendency for processes to become formalized (increase in unnecessary work, process areas, etc.) (8)
2	Heavy workload associated with appraisals (2)
3	Unsuited to small, short-duration projects
4	Top-down imposition of program exacerbates sense of coercion

(Figures in brackets indicate number of organizations that gave response)

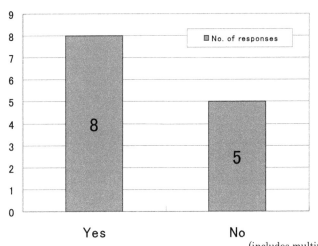

(includes multiple responses)

Fig. 2-10 Would you Recommend Other Organizations Seek CMMI?
－ Results of survey of organizations with CMMI level 5 (4) －

Table 2-7 Reasons for Recommending or not Recommending CMMI
－ Results of survey of organizations with CMMI level 5 (4) －

№	Reason for recommending CMMI
1	Because it enables comprehensive process improvement (3)
2	Can identify weaknesses
3	Helpful for solving problems
4	Able to benchmark own position relative to international standard

Note: Would recommend CMMI not for the purpose of achieving the
level, but only if genuine improvement could be achieved (2)

№	Reason for not recommending CMMI
1	Benefits do not justify cost (4)
2	Achieving the level tends to become the goal in itself (3)
3	Tendency for more tasks than necessary to be defined to achieve level

(Figures in brackets indicate number of organizations that gave response)

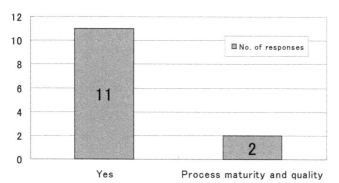

(includes multiple responses)

Fig. 2-11 Do Mature Processes Improve Quality?
— Results of survey of organizations with CMMI level 5 (5) —

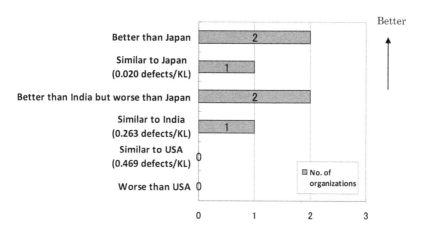

- Half of respondents replied
- Post-release defects: Defects within 12 months of release (defects/KLOC)

Fig. 2-12 Level of Post-Release Defects
— Results of survey of organizations with CMMI level 5 (5) —
(M. Cusumano et al., "Software Development Worldwide: The State of the Practice",
IEEE Software, Vol.20, No.6, pp.34-38, 2003)

Table 2-8 What are the Essential Factors for Improving Quality
— Results of survey of organizations with CMMI level 5 (6) —

№	Essential factors for improving quality
1	Emphasis on quality in the attitudes of team members and organizational culture (5)
2	Visualization and quantification of results and feedback (4)
3	Senior management leadership (3)
4	Reviews (3)
5	Ongoing checks (2)
6	An approach that seeks to reduce workloads (2)
7	Identification and deployment of best practice
8	Acquisition of basic technology for software development
9	Ensuring that processes are rigorously followed
10	Building in quality at each stage of development

(Figures in brackets indicate number of organizations that gave response)

Table 2-9 Technologies and Know-how that Aid Quality Improvement
— Results of survey of organizations with CMMI level 5 (6) —

№	Technologies and know-how that aid quality improvement	Category
1	Methods for project estimation (3)	Management technology
2	Accumulation of past data	
3	Track differences between estimates and actual results	
4	Management indices for reliability improvement (JISA)	
5	Development of management tools based on requirements management	Development technology
6	Standardization of development methods using PKG and frameworks, etc.	
7	Extreme derivative development process (XDDP)	
8	Review and inspection (3)	Review
9	Emphasize eradication of defects in upstream processes	
10	Test first	Testing
11	Coverage assessment during testing	
12	Visualization of conditions for performing testing (graphical)	
13	Static checking of source code	
14	Design review	Review or check by third party
15	Progress review by SQA	
16	Use of third party assessments	
17	"Naze naze" analysis (5 Whys)	"Naze naze" analysis and horizontal deployment
18	Horizontal deployment (Disseminate lessons from failed projects)	

(Figures in brackets indicate number of organizations that gave response)

Chapter 3. Software Quality Accounting

3.1 Introduction

NEC established its first organization specializing in software development in the year 1974. Until that point, the development of software had been one of the jobs of the hardware department. This period was before the dawn of modern software development, and with the subsequent spread of software to every area, the scale of software expanded until there was a major shortage of engineers, leading to fears of a "Software Crisis". In addition, dealing with the large number of defects in shipped software was becoming costly, and software quality problems started growing serious enough to represent a business challenge.

A number of Japanese corporations began working on improvements to deal with this software quality problem starting in the 1970s [3-1][3-2][3-3][3-4]. These efforts by Japanese corporations in securing software quality were made known to Europe and the US in the 1980s and 1990s, and garnered a certain level of recognition [3-5]. The efforts were characterized by an attempt to apply the statistical quality management techniques that had been so successful in Japanese hardware manufacturing business to software development as well.

In order to solve these quality problems in software development, NEC developed a wide range of efforts such as SWQC activities over the course of more than 20 years [3-6] [3-7] [3-8]. One of the techniques built as a result was "software quality accounting" [3-9] (referred to below as "quality accounting"). "Quality accounting" was invented around 1982 by a department developing operating systems and general-purpose middle software for use in NEC's IT products, and is a software quality management technique that is still being continuously improved to this day. The author of this dissertation played a central and continuous role in the construction and application of quality accounting in the organization that invented this technique (referred to below as "the organization that invented quality accounting"), and is currently responsible for quality assurance in the same organization. The organization that invented quality accounting was also NEC's first organization specializing in software development, as described in chapter 1. This chapter discusses software quality accounting.

3.2 Technique Overview

3.2.1 Quality Accounting System

Quality accounting is a software quality management technique that can be used to describe how quality is built into software using evidence that is certain. With quality accounting, detection threshold management based on the number of defects as plotted on the main axis can be used to achieve this goal. Therefore, with quality accounting, the number of defects injected during development must always be maintained as a highly precise estimated value. The "quality accounting system" shown in Fig. 3-1 is technology that is used to meet this requirement.

Quality accounting is comprised of the "defect count threshold management" and "defect count forecast and forecast update" techniques. In particular, there is a large number of "defect count forecast and forecast updates" which are used to revise the predicted number of defects based on a variety of different events that may occur during development.

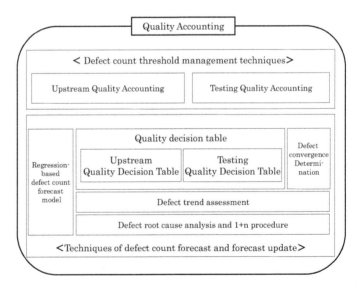

Fig. 3-1 Quality Accounting System

3.2.2   Development Process as Envisioned in Quality Accounting

The development processes envisioned in quality accounting follow the V model discussed in chapter 2 (see Fig. 2-2). Processes from basic design through coding are referred to as "upstream processes", and processes from unit tests through system tests are referred to as "testing processes". Each upstream process is comprised of "design" and "review" tasks, and the relationship between design and review is shown in Fig. 3-2. "Design" takes the specifications of the previous process (final version) as the output of the previous process and uses it as input until the design specifications (first version) of the current design process is complete. "Review" refers to all subsequent review tasks, which are repeated until the design specifications (final version) are complete. Defects are recognized during the process in which they occur, and measurement starts during the "review" of the process in question and on.

Quality accounting is applied by combining the different techniques shown in Fig. 3-1 based on the progress of development work (see Fig. 3-3).

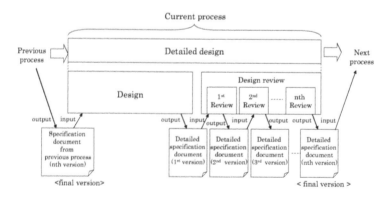

Fig. 3-2 The relation between "design" and "review" (Example of detailed design)

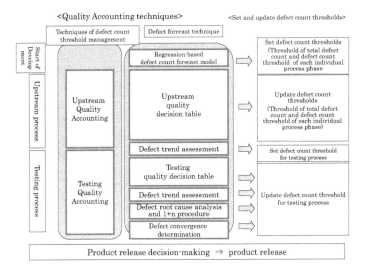

Fig. 3-3 Software development processes and the applicable Quality Accounting
Techniques

3.2.3 Scope of Application of Quality Accounting

Quality accounting is a technique that was built in a department responsible for developing operating systems for IT products and general-purpose middle software products. Since a general-purpose software product is developed with general uses by a wide range of customers in mind, rather than a specific set of customers, the software development department defines its own requirement specifications after analyzing trends in both technologies and customers. For this reason, as a rule there is no need for the coordination regarding specifications with important customers that occurs in the case of software developed for specific customers. Although these differences exist in the work required during software development based on the category of software, the work required starting with design is essentially the same. It is against this background that quality accounting is currently being applied throughout the NEC group as a standard quality management technique. Based on actual results, quality accounting can be applied within the following range:

· Assuming that the technique is applied to the waterfall model and other

44

plan-driven processes [3-10], it can be applied to development processes among the main life cycle processes defined in software life cycle processes (ISO/IEC12207/1995).

- Application does not depend on the software category, such as enterprise or embedded software products.

3.2.4   Characteristics of Quality Accounting

Quality accounting is based on the idea that defects should be seen as "debts". It is more economical to pay off debts early, before they grow due to accrued interest. Software defects are similar in the sense that the regression caused by each defect can be reduced if defects injected during design and coding can be quickly detected during reviewing or testing, before each single defect gives birth to multiple additional defects. The software is shipped after every debt is repaid, or in other words, after every defect is detected (for removal).

The basic idea behind quality accounting is to not inject defects, and to rapidly detect any defects that may have been injected. Based on this idea, the principle of upstream quality accounting is to detect any injected defects before the next process, and the principle of testing quality accounting is to ship after all injected defects have been detected (see Fig. 3-4). Quality accounting emphasizes defect detection during reviews as part of upstream processes, with a target upstream defect detection rate of 80%. The upstream defect detection rate refers to the percentage of all defects detected before shipping that are detected during the upstream processes.

Quality accounting is characterized by the following two points, which were conceived of and have been continuously improved in order to achieve the aforementioned principles:

- Early assurance of quality through the detection of defects during reviews
  - ➤ "Upstream quality accounting" manages defects detected during reviews in both defect injection and defect detection phases
- Precise exit criteria in software testing
  - ➤ Remaining issues are grasped and resolved by using a combination of the following three techniques: "defect trend assessment", "defect root cause analysis and 1+n procedure", and "defect convergence determination"

3.2.5   Procedures of Quality Accounting

Defect count threshold management is implemented after the start of development, with upstream quality accounting applied during upstream processes, and testing quality accounting applied during testing processes. Quality analysis is implemented regularly over a management span (for instance, weekly) in accordance with the procedures shown in Fig. 3-5. Since the management span would be too slow if it corresponded to the end of each process, it is important to grasp the situation during each process, and to implement appropriate countermeasures in real time whenever a problem occurs. At the end of a process there is only time to verify the results of dealing with a problem, and even if a countermeasure taken during the process is insufficient, it is often difficult to implement additional countermeasures.

As a result of quality analysis, it is determined whether or not the target level of quality has been built in, and defect count thresholds are revised as necessary. The applied quality analysis techniques differ somewhat between upstream and testing processes. Since software is built during the upstream processes, the "defect root cause analysis during each injection phase" that is focused on during the defect's injection phase is implemented. A defect's injection phase is the process during which that defect was injected, or in other words, one of the upstream processes in the development processes of the V model shown in Fig. 2-2. Quality is determined throughout the upstream and testing processes using a "quality decision table". During a testing process, once the planned testing is almost completely finished, remaining issues are grasped and resolved by using a combination of the following three techniques in order to verify exit criteria in software testing: "defect trend assessment", "defect root cause analysis and 1+n procedure", and "defect convergence determination".

```
Principle of Quality Accounting
• Do not inject defects. Rapidly detect any injected defects.

Principle of Upstream Quality Accounting
• Detect any injected defects before the next process.
    – Removal rate of 80% in defect injection phase
    – Detect remaining 20% in next process

Principle of Testing Quality Accounting
• Ship after all injected defects have been detected.


Target
• Upstream defect detection rate of 80%.
```

Fig. 3-4 Principles of Quality Accounting

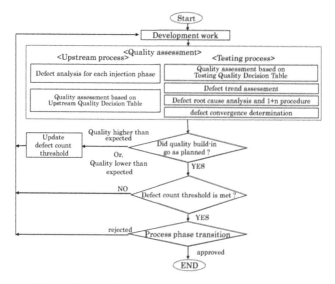

Fig. 3-5 The workflow of Upstream Quality Accounting

3.3 Methods of Applying Quality Accounting to Upstream Processes

At the start of development, a regression-based defect count forecast model is applied in order to set the defect count threshold representing the number of defects that are predicted to be injected during this development. Quality accounting is applied during the upstream processes after the start of development, according to the quality accounting procedures shown in Fig. 3-5.

3.3.1 Setting Defect count thresholds at Start of Development

A "regression-based defect count forecast model" is applied in order to predict the defect count. This regression-based defect count forecast model as it currently exists has been continuously improved based on the COCOMO model [3-11] and on-site requirements. The regression-based defect count forecast model used in quality accounting is as shown below:

$$B = C \cdot \prod_{i=1}^{n} \alpha_i \cdot S, \qquad (3\text{-}1)$$

B : defect forecast value (number of defects),

C : standard defect count ,

α_i : influence factor affecting defects $(i=1,2,...,n)$,

S : development scale (KLOC)

In the above formula (3-1), the defect forecast value is essentially derived by multiplying the development scale by the standard defect count (constant), and is adjusted by the influence factor affecting defects. C is a constant that is derived through multiple regression analysis. The influence factor affecting defects α_i is used by selecting i, which is a factor indicating how strong the effect is on the defect count $(i=1,2,...,n)$. Based on considerations of past performance and how easy it is to apply on-site, quality accounting has adopted, as a rule, two influence factors at present: the developer's "technology of development team" and development's "difficultness of the development target software". These influence factors are evaluated in five stages, and the numerical values used in each of these stages are set based on the results of statistical analysis. An example of defect forecast values calculated based on the regression-based defect count forecast model is shown in Fig. 3-6.

An example of improvements made to facilitate easy on-site application is shown. The "technology of development team", which is one of the influence factors affecting defects, was originally represented as a matrix in order to quantify the years of experience of each engineer, rather than a five-stage evaluation scale. It was discovered, however, that the number of years of development experience is unrelated to the "technology of development team" factor. There was, however a strong demand from on-site project managers in charge of development projects for the ability to reflect their outlook on the development projects in the defect forecast. Based on this history, the "technology of development team" was switched to a five-stage evaluation system, and that is the method currently being used by project managers.

The formula (3-1), which is a regression model, is derived using data from the past that is accumulated for each middle software, operating system, or other software product. The reason it is created separately for each software product is that each product has different attributes due to the project, the software, or other factors.

Furthermore, the "target defect count ratio for each process phase" is set while referring to the aforementioned past data, and giving consideration to the current development improvement targets. The target defect count ratio for each process phase is set in order to achieve an upstream defect detection rate of 80%, as a rule. The "defect count threshold" for each defect detection phase is set by capitalizing on the target defect count ratio for each process phase, for the defect forecast value calculated using formula (3-1) (see Fig. 3-7) .

3.3.2 Defect Injection and Detection

Quality accounting manages defects separately in a defect injection phase and a defect detection phase. This idea of injection and detection is particularly important in upstream quality accounting. Fig. 3-8 shows examples of this defect injection and detection.

Defects are injected in the design or coding of upstream processes, and are detected during reviewing or testing. How precisely the defect injection phase of defects can be determined is one of the key points that affect how effective the application of quality accounting can be. In the case of a developer with a low technology level, sometimes the developer will be confused by the act of correcting the program, and will see almost all defects as coding defects. If there are a large number of defects injected during the coding process, then it will be necessary to reconfirm the defect injection phase. In general, the more upstream the design process, the higher the technology level of the responsible developer, and the fewer the mistakes there will be in determining the defect injection phase. The more downstream the process, the more frequently developers at a wide range of different levels will be involved, and so it will be necessary to always pay attention to the appropriateness of determinations of the defect injection phase. If many mistakes are made in the determination of the defect injection phase, then a risk of mistaken determinations of the state of quality will ensue.

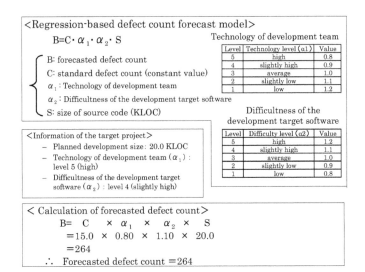

<Regression-based defect count forecast model>

$$B = C \cdot \alpha_1 \cdot \alpha_2 \cdot S$$

- B: forecasted defect count
- C: standard defect count (constant value)
- α_1 : Technology of development team
- α_2 : Difficultness of the development target software
- S: size of source code (KLOC)

Technology of development team

Level	Technology level ($\alpha 1$)	Value
5	high	0.8
4	slightly high	0.9
3	average	1.0
2	slightly low	1.1
1	low	1.2

Difficultness of the development target software

Level	Difficulty level ($\alpha 2$)	Value
5	high	1.2
4	slightly high	1.1
3	average	1.0
2	slightly low	0.9
1	low	0.8

<Information of the target project>
- Planned development size: 20.0 KLOC
- Technology of development team (α_1) : level 5 (high)
- Difficultness of the development target software (α_2) : level 4 (slightly high)

< Calculation of forecasted defect count>

$$B = C \times \alpha_1 \times \alpha_2 \times S$$
$$= 15.0 \times 0.80 \times 1.10 \times 20.0$$
$$= 264$$

∴ Forecasted defect count $= 264$

Fig. 3-6 Example of Defect Forecast Values Calculated
Using Regression-Based Defect Count Forecast Model

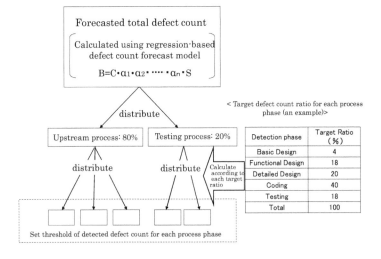

Forecasted total defect count

Calculated using regression-based defect count forecast model

$$B = C \cdot \alpha_1 \cdot \alpha_2 \cdot \cdots \cdot \alpha_n \cdot S$$

distribute

Upstream process: 80%   Testing process: 20%

distribute   distribute   Calculate according to each target ratio

Set threshold of detected defect count for each process phase

< Target defect count ratio for each process phase (an example)>

Detection phase	Target Ratio (%)
Basic Design	4
Functional Design	18
Detailed Design	20
Coding	40
Testing	18
Total	100

Fig. 3-7 Setting defect count threshold for each process phase

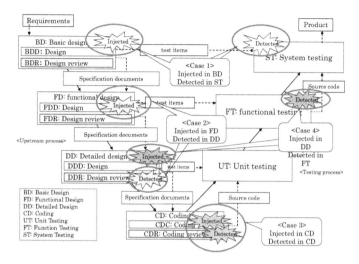

Fig. 3-8 Injection and detection of defects (an example)

3.3.3 Defect Analysis for Each Injection Phase

"Defect analysis for each injection phase" is used to organize data in the format of each review implementation (see Fig. 3-9). This analysis is conducted from the following three perspectives:

(1) Trend in count of detected defects as compared to number of reviews
- If the total defect count increases or remains flat as the number of reviews increases, then there is the risk that continuing reviewing without making a change may not produce results. If this happens, temporarily halt reviewing and analyze the cause.

(2) State of detection of defects injected during previous processes
- In rough terms, the target values for achieving the principles of quality accounting are 80% detection during the defect injection phase (process), with the remaining 20% detected during the next process. If injected defects are detected in the previous process in excess of these target values, then the work output of the previous process is determined to have a poor level of built-in quality, and focus returns to the previous process in order to verify its work output.
- If the target values of 80% detected in the defect injection phase and 20%

detected in the next process are achieved, then any defects remaining after the upstream processes are complete are seen as the just 20% of defects injected during the coding process. In this way, the quality accounting target of an "upstream defect detection rate of 80%" can be reliably achieved.

(3) State of detection of defects injected upstream from the previous process

- According to the principles of quality accounting, any defects injected upstream from the previous process should already have been detected. In spite of this, if defects are still detected that were injected upstream from the previous process, then the work output of the defect injection phase is determined to have a poor level of quality, and the work output of that defect injection phase must be verified.

By analyzing from the three viewpoints described above, it is possible to detect and handle quality problems in the work output of processes earlier and further upstream than the process in question. In particular, the results obtained by (2) and (3) are problems injected during the design stage of the upstream process, and so in many cases they will generally not be discovered until the integration testing or later. The ability to detect these problems in upstream processes is one of the major advantages of quality accounting. Also, since a process that injects a large number of defects is a weak point for that project, by focusing on resolving problem points in that process, it is expected that this will result in a major improvement in quality.

3.3.4   Quality Analysis Using Quality Decision Tables

Quality decision tables come in two types, upstream quality decision tables and testing quality decision tables. A quality decision table is used to analyze the state of the detected defect count during review or test efforts, and makes it possible to determine actual quality results as compared to expectations for the current point in time according to the plan. Review effort is used for the upstream processes, and a test effort is used for the testing processes. In addition, defect count threshold update formulas are provided for updating defect count thresholds (see Fig. 3-10) .

Current process phase：detailed design

	Detailed design	Detailed design 1st Review	Detailed design 2nd Review	....	Detailed design Nth Review	Total
Basic design defect	0	0	2		0	2
Functional design defect	8	2	5		0	18
Detailed design defect	-	13	16		5	38
total	8	15	23		5	58
grand total	8	23	46		58	-

1. Defect count decreasing as the project is repeatedly reviewed ?
2. Are there many defects detected that were injected in the previous process phase ?
3. Are there any defects detected that were injected in process phases further upstream than the previous process phase?

Fig. 3-9 Data chart for defect analysis for each injection phase (an example)

Quality Decision Table		Review effort per KLOC or Testing effort per KLOC		
		result < planned − n%	Planned −n% <= result <= planned +n%	planned + n% < result
Defects detected during review per KLOC or Defects detected during testing per KLOC	Result<planned − n%	Not ready for quality decision·making ⇒ Continue review	Quality better than planned ⇒Update threshold with Calculation Formula 1	Quality better than planned ⇒Update threshold with Calculation Formula 2
	Planned·n% <= result <= planned + n%	Quality is lower than planned ⇒Update threshold with Calculation Formula 1	Quality is as planned	Quality is as planned
	Planned + n%<result	Quality is lower than planned ⇒Update threshold with Calculation Formula 1	Quality is lower than planned ⇒Update threshold with Calculation Formula 1	Quality is lower than planned ⇒Update threshold with Calculation Formula 2

<Calculation Formula for defect count threshold update>

(1) Formula:
New threshold for total defect count

$$= \text{previous threshold} \times \frac{\dfrac{\text{Actual number of defects detected during review (or testing)}}{\text{Actual hours spent for review (or testing)}}}{\dfrac{\text{Planned for defects detected during review (or testing)}}{\text{Planned for hours spent for review (or testing)}}}$$

(2) Formula:
New threshold for total defect count

$$= \text{previous threshold} \times \frac{\text{Actual number of defects detected during review (or testing) per KLOC}}{\text{Planned for defects detected during review (or testing) per KLOC}}$$

Fig. 3-10 Quality Decision Table

Planned values are set for review and test efforts using a separately provided regression effort forecast model. The threshold a% in the quality decision table is set according to the organization's capabilities, with 20% as standard. When the actual application time of quality accounting is short, management precision tends to be low as the actual dispersion relative to the plan is large, and so "a" is set to a large value. Quality analysis using a quality decision table is often conducted at the end of each process. When it is conducted during a process, the quality decision table's planned value is multiplied by a value representing the percent of progress.

If it is assumed that the reviewing and testing methods are the same as in the past, then the review and test efforts represent the level of energy expended on defect detection, and the number of detected defects represent the results of reviewing or testing. The aim of quality analysis using a quality decision table is to grasp and respond to changes in quality that occur during development, and which were not considered during planning. These "changes" are thought to appear most often in the state of reviewing or testing. Ideas for ways to grasp these changes include the following:

· If the quality is as planned, then the actual numbers of defects detected during review and test efforts should correspond to the planned values when measured.

· If the quality is worse than planned, then the actual numbers of defects detected during planned review or test efforts should be larger.

· If the quality is better than planned, then the actual numbers of defects detected during planned review or test efforts should be smaller.

Based on the result of grasping this "change", the defect count threshold update formula shown in Fig. 3-10 is used to revise the defect count threshold as necessary. Two formulas are provided for updating the defect count threshold, based on the past results of application on-site. Formula (1) is a revision method that, when it is assumed that the review and test methods do not differ from those used in the past, treats the ratio of the actual value to the target value of the detected defect count per unit time for the review or test effort as a ratio indicating the quality actually built in as compared with the planned quality. If the actual review or test effort results significantly surpass what was planned, then this is taken as evidence that the review or test method has changed, and the idea behind formula (1) does not apply. In this case, as shown in formula (2), built-in quality is thought to be represented by the detected defect count per unit time, and the ratio of the actual value to that target value is seen as representing the ratio of built-in quality with respect to the planned quality, and the threshold is updated.

A wide range of events can occur during software development, including major changes to requirement specifications, increased scale of development, replaced development project members, and so on. The idea behind quality analysis using a quality decision table represents the basic idea behind the quality analysis of quality accounting itself. Quality analysis at the site of development must bear this basic idea in mind while considering each separate development condition.

3.4   Methods of Applying Quality Accounting in Testing Processes

The test defect count threshold is set based on the remaining test defect count as forecast at the start of the testing process. The defect count threshold for testing process is a numerical value calculated by subtracting the number of defects detected in the upstream processes from the defect count threshold. As during the upstream processes, quality accounting is applied during the testing processes based on the quality accounting procedures shown in Fig. 3-4. Quality management is implemented around the core of quality analysis, based on the testing quality decision table during testing processes. The explanations in this chapter focused on the exit criteria in software testing, which is a characteristic of quality accounting. The "defect root cause analysis and 1+n procedure" that is applied in testing process exit criteria is the most important technique used, and is also an effective way to make systematic improvements, so it is discussed in detail in the next chapter after an overview in this chapter.

3.4.1   Exit Criteria in Software Testing Using Quality Accounting

In quality accounting, the end of planned testing does not mean that testing is complete. Experience shows that planned testing alone tends to overlook something at an extremely high frequency. Quality is analyzed when the planned testing is almost complete, and it is necessary to work towards grasping and resolving any remaining issues as the product is brought up to a shippable quality level. To this end, with quality accounting, the three techniques of "defect trend assessment", "defect root cause analysis and 1+n procedure", and "defect convergence determination" are used together near the end of testing.

During "defect trend assessment", all defects detected during testing are analyzed from a variety of different angles, so that any issue overlooked during design, review, or testing can be understood along with weak points in development, and so that additional reviewing and testing can be implemented. During the "defect root cause analysis and 1+n procedure", major defects detected during and after system testing are focused on, and the causes of injection and overlooking are analyzed in order to grasp small overlooked details and problems that occur during work. Additional reviewing and testing is then conducted based on these analyses. The results of these additional reviews and tests are once again analyzed for quality, and if any new remaining issues are detected, then further reviews and tests are repeated. With "defect convergence determination", on the other hand, by analyzing the trend in the cumulative defect total as compared to the test execution rate over the entire testing process, convergence is determined. As a result of quality analysis conducted using these three techniques, when all concerned parties agree that there is no problem in any of the results, it is determined that there are no more remaining issues, and testing ends. This is the "exit criteria in software testing method" in quality accounting.

3.4.2   Defect Trend Assessment

"Defect trend assessment" is an analysis technique that classifies and observes detected defects from a variety of different analytical viewpoints. In addition to application at the point where planned testing is mostly finished, application of this technique also occurs during quality analysis when upstream processing finishes. The setting of the analytical viewpoint according to the attributes of the software being analyzed affects the analysis level of defect trend assessment. Quality accounting organizes standard analytical viewpoints (Table 3-1).

For instance, by normalizing the number of defects for each function of the software being analyzed for the development scale, it becomes possible to compare defect counts per unit time for each function in order to extract functions with a large number of defects. Furthermore, by grouping defects according to the customer's severity level classification, it is possible to compare defects per function from the customer's perspective. By assigning priority rankings based on the results and implementing quality improvement measures for each function, it is possible to achieve effective quality improvements. By adding additional analytical viewpoints based on the details of the individual software products being analyzed to those in Table 3-1, it becomes possible to implement quality analysis that is even more persuasive.

Fig. 3-11 shows an example of defect trend assessment. This is an example of the analysis of defects detected during function and system tests, from the end of planned system testing. After four types of defect trend assessments, the conclusion is that additional verification will be required of the three types of defect causes of injection in function B-2. This is only one example, however, and it is important to note that the same analysis cannot simply be applied to any analyzed software product.

Table 3-1 The view points of Defect Trend Assessment

Viewpoints of analysis	Contents
Normalization	Normalize the defect count using units such as size of source code. The defect count is affected by the source code size, but by using the defect count per unit size, it is possible to compare the numbers.
Software functions	Group the defects according to the corresponding software function. Possible to capture which software function has a large defect count
Defect injection phase	Categorize the detected defect by injection phase. Possible to understand which process phase such as design, coding had the problem.
Severity of defect	Categorize the defects by the impact to the user (Critical, serious, negligible, and others). Be able to acknowledge if there are any serious defects happening.
Cause of defect injection	Categorize the defects by the cause of injection. The common causes of injection are such as design mistake, missing considerations, simple mistake, work step corruption, not enough understanding of specification, and degrade. When initially defining the list of possible injection causes that the engineers will use in their review work, the list need to be chosen/adjusted to match the characteristics of the assessment target software.
Condition for the defect to happen	Categorize defect by the condition for the corresponding defect to happen (normal flow of program execution, exception handlings, timing, combinations, limit values).
Damage caused by the defect	Categorize defects by the damage caused by the defect (abnormal results, system failure, data crash, and others).
Injectee (injected by)	Categorize the detected defect by the injectee (injected by). Possible to capture the defect count of defects unintentionally injected.

3.4.3   Defect Root Cause Analysis and 1+n Procedure

With the "defect root cause analysis and 1+n procedure" technique, the root causes behind each single defect being injected and overlooked are analyzed, and additional reviews and tests are conducted regarding those root causes in order to detect same-type defects (see Fig. 3-12). A "same-type defect" is a defect that was injected or overlooked due to the same cause as another defect. As "n" of same-type defects are detected for a single defect, the additional reviews and tests for that root cause are referred to as the "1+n procedure".

The "defect root cause analysis and 1+n procedure" technique is applied for important

1. Defect analysis for each injection phase

Many defects including functional design defect are detected in function B-2.

< Defects injected at each software function(From Functional Testing to System testing)>

Defect injection phase	Function: B-1	Function: B-2	Function: B-3	Total for Function B
Basic Design defect	0	0	0	0
Functional Design defect	0	2	0	2
Detailed Design defect	0	3	1	4
Coding defect	1	15	4	20
Total	1	20	5	26

2. Analysis of defect count normalized by development size

The size of function B-2 is large with large number of defects, because B-2 function realize the core of B function. Functional Design defects were previously detected as well.

<Defects per KLOC for each function (FT to ST)>

	Function: B-1	Function: B-2	Function: B-3	Total for Function B
Size of source code (KLOC)	2.9	15.3	7.2	25.4
Defects (Counts/KLOC)	0.34	1.31	0.69	1.02

3. Analysis of defect count for each Severity level classification

Regarding defect classification by priority and severity, B-2 function has 2 critical and 8 major defects.

→Therefore it was decided to execute quality analysis specifically for B-2 function.

<Severity level classification for each detailed function (FT to ST)>

Severity level	Function: B-1	Function: B-2	Function: B-3	Total for Function
Critical	0	2	0	2
Serious	0	8	1	9
Negligible	1	10	4	15
Total	1	20	5	26

4. Defect analysis for each cause of injection of B-2 function

Conclusion: Need to additionally check B-2 function in the following aspects

Result of Test enforcement for GUI

<Defect classification by cause of injection of B-2 function (FT to ST)>

Cause for defect injection	Defect injection phase				
	Basic Design defect	Functional Design defect	Detailed Design defect	Coding defect	Total
Incorrectly defined GUI display format			1	8	9
Not enough care taken in interface design		2	1	3	6
Not enough care taken for abnormal conditions			1	4	5
Total	0	2	3	15	20

The engineer that knows the overall function of B happened to be out of office for FD review. It should have been covered by other reviews but ...

The number includes one defect detected during 3rd party evaluation (evaluation by QA team)

Fig. 3-11 Example of Defect Trend Analysis at End of System Testing

(Defects detected during function and system tests are subject to analysis.)

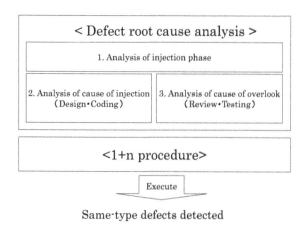

Fig. 3-12   Defect root cause analysis and 1+n procedure

defects detected during and after system tests during development. Also, as a quality improvement measure, the "defect root cause analysis and 1+n procedure" technique is applied for all defects after shipment. Refer to the next chapter for details regarding the "defect root cause analysis and 1+n procedure" technique.

3.4.4   Defect Convergence Determination

"Defect convergence determination" is a method that was invented in order to apply a software reliability growth model [3-12] on-site (see Fig. 3-13). By focusing on the trend during the final stage of testing, it is possible to achieve a unique on-site convergence determination. The testing trend is the slope of the reliability growth curve using the cumulative detected defect count as compared with the test item count. The range for the final stage of testing is based on a standard of the last 80% to 100% with the total number of test items as 100. Specific settings are based on the actual software being analyzed.

The defect convergence rate calculated with formula (3-2) below is used during defect convergence determination:

$\alpha = \triangle 1 \diagup \triangle 0,$ 　　　(3-2)

　　α : defect convergence rate,

　　$\triangle 1$: detected defect count during final stage of testing/test item count during final stage of testing,

　　$\triangle 0$: detected defect count during entire test/test item count during entire test.

The defect convergence rate α calculated with formula (3-2) is compared with a convergence threshold prepared separately, and if the result is within the threshold, then convergence is determined to have occurred. This convergence threshold is set based on an analysis of the relationship between defect convergence rates and quality after shipment for that organization's past projects, and is a value based on experience, which is derived from each separate organization's stored data. The convergence threshold is generally a value smaller than 0.5.

An analysis method using a software reliability growth model is well-known as a means of determining defect convergence [3-12]. With this method, the result of convergence determination will differ depending on the model used as well as how that model is applied. For this reason, at sites of development that are required to maintain a constant level of quality, improvement of application methods was necessary. Defect convergence determination for use in quality accounting was invented to solve this problem, and the same result is achieved regardless of who does the determination.

During quality accounting, quality is analyzed when planned testing is almost finished, and additional tests are necessary in order to deal with remaining issues. Therefore, the final stage of testing, which is the subject of this defect convergence determination, is used to determine the state of these additional tests.

3.5　Emphasizing a Hands-on Approach

A hands-on approach emphasizes "visiting the location of the trouble, looking at the actual objects, and observing what is really happening" instead of sitting at one's desk theorizing. Quality accounting strongly requires the implementation of a hands-on approach.

Quality accounting implements quality management based on data. Application of quality accounting requires the verification of actual events as they occur on-site, rather than simply relying on measured data, which carries the risk of mistaken perception of facts. In upstream processes, it is important to verify design specifications, review records, and other actual work output, as well as design details, how detailed design specification descriptions are, the suitability of reviewers, the details of reviews and defects detected by those reviews, and other factors. The state of quality assurance is determined during the testing process by verifying test specifications, test results, test programs, and so on, as well as the details of actually detected defects. Regardless of the stage of development, it is extremely important to verify human elements on-site, such as developer motivation and teamwork.

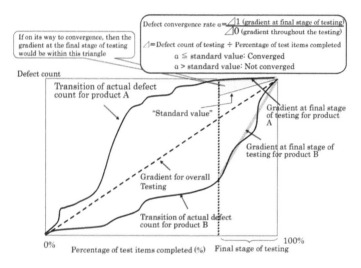

Fig. 3-13 The concept of Defect Convergence Determination

The results of verifying the development site are combined with the results of analyzing data acquired by applying quality accounting techniques, true causal relationships are analyzed, and the state of quality is determined. If the results of verifying the state of the development site do not match the results of data-based quality analysis, then the causes of this discrepancy is also analyzed. New problems that have never been seen before are always potentially cropping up in software development due to a variety of events and new technological elements. It is possible to rapidly discover problems caused by new factors such as these by verifying the site of development. Methods of measuring new factors can also be invented if necessary. This has driven the evolution of quality accounting.

3.6 Conclusion

This chapter provided an overview of quality accounting and described the technique as well as methods for applying it. Quality accounting is a technique that was born on the site of software development as a means of resolving software quality problems, and has been constructed over more than 20 years of repeated revision based on application results. Therefore, it is a technology that has been validated at the site of software development.

Quality accounting presupposes the waterfall model or other plan-driven processes, and can be applied regardless of whether the software is enterprise software, embedded software, or some other category. Quality accounting is characterized by 1) early quality assurance through the detection of defects during reviews, and 2) precise exit criteria in software testing. By implementing detection threshold management for the defects injected during software development, quality accounting is a quality management technique that can be used to describe how quality is reliably built in, with a target upstream defect detection rate of 80% for the ratio between the detected defect count during reviews and the total detected defect count before shipment. Details regarding the effects of applying quality accounting are described in chapter 7. Quality accounting has grown into a standard quality management technique that is being applied by 60,000 software development engineers in the NEC group.

Chapter 4. Defect Root Cause Analysis and 1+n Procedure

4.1 Introduction

In order to assure software quality and improve processes at the site of software development, the root causes of any problems that occur are sometimes analyzed, and efforts are taken to resolve these root causes. This root cause analysis technique is well-known by names such as the "five whys analysis". "Five whys analysis" is one technique that is often used on-site, but it is actually not very effective at reaching the root cause when applied, and often winds up simply listing the developers' areas of dissatisfaction.

This chapter describes the quality accounting technique "defect root cause analysis and 1+n procedure" in concrete terms, and discusses the characteristics and effects of this technique based on application examples. "Defect root cause analysis and 1+n procedure" is a defect cause analysis technique that has been optimized for software development, and it resolves the issues of five whys analysis. In quality accounting, five whys analysis is called "defect root cause analysis". Defect root cause analysis is a technique that is also an effective means of process improvement, and is a technology that is indispensable for achieving high-quality software development.

4.2 Relationship between "Defect Root Cause Analysis and 1+n Procedure" and Related Techniques

The Toyota "five whys" method is the most famous root cause analysis technique [4-1]. The root cause is reached by repeating "why?" five times. It is a scientific approach that emphasizes facts while seeking to discern the causal relationships between them as well as the hidden true factors behind them. The Toyota "five whys" technique is not limited to software development, but is widely and generally applied. For this reason, a variety of different application types are seen based on considerations of the attributes of each area of application.

PNA (Process Network Analysis) is proposed as a root cause analysis technique for use in software development [4-2]. This technique strongly focuses on the processes of software development, and is characterized by analysis that is always aware of management processes.

In addition, there are techniques that focus on failure modes in their cause analyses for the sake of product reliability assurance, including FTA (Fault Tree Analysis) and FMEA (Failure Mode and Effects Analysis) [2-12]. These techniques are also applied to software development. FTA and FMEA are also a type of root analysis technique as they analyze root causes.

The most widespread techniques in use at software development sites must be the Toyota "five whys" technique and applied versions of the same. Although these techniques vary somewhat in how they focus on causal relationships while repeating the question "why", they all share in common the method of tracing back to the root cause by repeating "why". Therefore, this dissertation collectively refers to the Toyota "five whys" technique and all of its variants as "five whys analysis" below.

Additional tests are sometimes conducted in order to improve the quality of software both before and after shipment, based on the results of defect analysis using the five whys technique for software development. This defect detection process through additional testing based on the root causes of defects is referred to as a "lateral search for defects". The goal of a lateral search for defects is to detect remaining defects with the same root cause as the original defects. For instance, if the root cause of a defect is insufficient research of technology documentation, then the goal of lateral search for defects would be the detection of other defects injected due to the same insufficient research of technology documentation.

Since the lateral search for defects technique appears simple at first glance, it is frequently used at sites of software development. Unfortunately, it is still difficult to analyze the root causes of defects and efficiently detect latent defects. The reasons for this difficulty lie in defect root cause analysis. It is rare that a defect has only one root cause, and in almost all cases, multiple causes exist for a defect [4-1]. For this reason, the more five whys analysis is conducted, the more causes branch out and appear to diverge, making it difficult to identify root causes.

Defect root causes can be grouped into two classifications, specific root causes and shared root causes. A specific root cause is the direct cause behind that defect being injected and overlooked. For instance, this includes design mistakes caused by missing technological information, or things that were overlooked in the writing of the design specifications that cause testing process items to be overlooked in turn. A shared root cause, on the other hand, is an indirect cause of that defect being injected and overlooked. Shared root causes include causes such as a lack of education or insufficient organizational standards. When preventive measures are taken against the specific root cause of a defect, the same type of defects should no longer be injected or overlooked after the measures are implemented. If preventive measures are taken against a defect's shared root cause, however, since the measures are indirect, even after they are implemented, there is no reliable guarantee that the same type of defect will not be injected or overlooked again in the future. Preventive measures addressing shared root causes can reduce the probability that defects of the same type will be injected and overlooked again, but they cannot prevent them with certainty. Therefore, lateral searches for defects must be done to address specific root causes, not shared root causes. Five whys analysis makes no distinction between specific and shared root causes.

The defect root cause analysis in the "defect root cause analysis and 1+n procedure" technique is a means of analyzing specific root causes. The "defect root cause analysis and 1+n procedure" technique improved the root cause analysis method based on five whys analysis so that specific root causes could be analyzed more reliably. This revision makes the technique a more effective way to conduct lateral searches for defects.

4.3   Overview of the "Defect Root Cause Analysis and 1+n Procedure" Technique

4.3.1   Relationship with Quality Accounting

As described in chapter 3, quality accounting has the following two characteristics:
- Early assurance of quality through the detection of defects during reviews
  - ➤ "Upstream quality accounting" manages defects detected during reviews in both defect injection and defect detection phases
- Precise exit criteria in software testing
  - ➤ Remaining issues are grasped and resolved by using a combination of the following three techniques: "defect trend assessment", "defect root cause analysis and 1+n procedure", and "defect convergence determination"

The "defect root cause analysis and 1+n procedure" is a technique that is used to implement the second characteristic of quality accounting, "exit criteria in software testing". With exit criteria in software testing, determination is based on analyses from the following three perspectives at the end of planned testing. Testing is complete when evaluations based on all three perspectives determine that there is no problem.

- The "defect trend assessment" technique is used to analyze whether or not anything is overlooked in systematic test viewpoints.
- The "defect root cause analysis and 1+n procedure" technique is used to analyze whether or not anything is overlooked in detailed test viewpoints.
- The "defect convergence determination" technique is used to analyze whether or not the probability of more actual defects being detected is low.

The "defect root cause analysis and 1+n procedure" is conducted on severe defects detected during the final stage of testing. It is thought that the existence of severe defects in the final stage of testing indicates the risk of something having been overlooked during previous development work. The "defect root cause analysis and 1+n procedure" was developed in order to enable the analysis of whether or not something was overlooked in these kinds of detailed test viewpoints.

4.3.2   Basic Idea

The "defect root cause analysis and 1+n procedure" technique analyzes the specific root cause of a single defect, and based on that specific root cause, seeks to detect other defects of the same type as the original defect. A "same-type defect" is a defect that is still hidden in the software due to the same specific root cause as the one that resulted in the original defect.

This technique uses the idea of a defect's "defect injection phase". A defect's injection phase is the process during which that defect was injected, or one of the upstream development processes in the V model shown in Fig. 2-2 of chapter 2. The specific root causes of this technique are limited to the following three types:

- The cause of a defect being injected in the design of that defect's defect injection phase (referred to as the "causes of injection" below)
- The cause of a defect being overlooked in the review of that defect's defect injection phase (referred to as the "cause of overlook during review" below)
- The cause of a defect being overlooked during the testing process (referred to as the "cause of overlook during testing" below)

The reason this technique limits specific root causes to the ones listed above is that its goal is to detect defects with the same type as the original defect. The direct cause for other defects of the same type being hidden in the software is limited to these three types of specific root causes.

The reason for this is that defects are injected during one of the upstream processes of

66

the V model. Also, defects are only detected by the "defect root cause analysis and 1+n procedure" during the review of the process in question or testing processes corresponding to that design process. The V model is characterized by the visual manifestation of corresponding design and test processes. If the injecting process can be identified through application of the V model, then it can be determined that the testing process during which the defect was overlooked is the corresponding testing process in the V model. The reason this technique presupposes use of the V model is that the V model is suited to the identification of defect injection and detection phases/processes.

In addition to specific root causes, a variety of different shared root causes affecting the development process are conceivable, such as engineer skill and team communication. These causes are not limited to a single defect, however, but rather are shared by other latent defects as well. These kinds of shared root causes are not treated as root causes by this technique because if they were, a wide range of root causes would have to be handled, and it would no longer be possible to precisely establish the focus of detection of same-type defects.

The "defect root cause analysis" part of the "defect root cause analysis and 1+n procedure" technique analyzes the three aforementioned specific root causes. The "1+n procedure" formulates additional reviews, test ranges, and details based on the results of "defect root cause analysis", and these additions are then used to detect same-type defects. The "1" in "1+n procedure" indicates how a single defect is subject to analysis, whereas the "n" indicates the number of same-type defects detected ($n \geq 1$). The name "1+n procedure" refers to how n same-type defects remain hidden when one defect is detected, and how these "n" latent same-type defects must also be detected. "Defect root cause analysis" and "1+n procedure" are both applied together as a set, thus the name "defect root cause analysis and 1+n procedure".

4.3.3   Application Method

The "defect root cause analysis and 1+n procedure" technique has the following characteristics:

- Since this is a technique for detecting same-type defects by analyzing the specific root causes of defects, it is suited for use in pinpoint correction of problems.
- Defect root cause analysis takes a fixed length of time.

For this reason, it is efficient to limit the application of this technique to severe problems only, and therefore it is mainly applied to severe problems in the final stage of testing, and to severe design mistakes. It is also applied to defects detected by the customer after shipment.

Defect root cause analysis is conducted for a single severe defect by analyzing root causes from the three viewpoints of "defect injection phase", "causes of injection", and "cause of overlook". Next, based on the results of this defect root cause analysis, the 1+n procedure is formulated to detect "n" same-type defects, and same-type defects are then detected.

4.3.4   Application Examples

In order to make the effects of "defect root cause analysis and 1+n procedure" easy to understand, this section describes an example of the technique's application (see Fig. 4-1).

This example is for a defect in threshold limit value processing. Threshold limit value processing defects are a problem that often occurs in software. In cases such as this, additional testing is often performed on other threshold limit value processing parts in order to verify the validity of that processing. It is expected that other same-type defects will be occur in threshold limit value processing.

As Fig. 4-1 indicates, however, the development history shows that this defect is actually due to a problem caused by an unexpected switch in engineers that occurred at the end of detail design process. This defect's specific root cause was not a simple mistake of threshold limit value processing implementation, but rather the existence of undocumented specifications that were only known to the previous engineer. Undocumented specifications are specifications that only exist inside the engineer's head, and are not documented in the design specifications. The same-type defects in Fig. 4-1 originated in undocumented specifications. Since only the previous engineer knows whether or not other undocumented specifications exist, it will be necessary for the previous engineer to review the scope of coding done by the new engineer in the 1+n procedure. The goal of this review is the detection of any other undocumented specifications that may have been left out of the design specifications. In this way, specific root causes can be analyzed that are not discoverable simply through an examination of surface-level events, as this technique is able to detect same-type defects.

On the other hand, the existence of undocumented specifications is a problem that may occur in any organization. The level of details to be included in design specification documents must be decided by each organization based on the technology level of that organization's engineers, as well as the level of knowledge the engineers possess in that area of development. The problem of the level of details included in documented design specifications can be a shared root cause that occurs in other projects as well. With five whys analysis, at the same time as the unexpected switch in engineers that was the specific root cause, the level of detail in the documented design specifications that is the shared root cause is also analyzed as one root cause. During five whys analysis, the further analysis proceeds, the more causes branch out, and multiple root causes are reached. In the stage before shipment as shown in this example, the specific root cause is analyzed in order to assure shipment quality, and same-type defects must be detected efficiently. Since five whys analysis does not differentiate between specific root causes and shared root causes, it is not very efficient. The "defect root cause analysis and 1+n procedure" technique solves this problem in five whys analysis, and has been constantly refined so that it can efficiently detect same-type defects.

4.3.5   Defect Injection Phase

The defect injection phase is analyzed before defect root cause analysis. In order to make it possible to identify the defect injection phase, the designed details must be clearly defined for each design process in the development processes.

Depending on the details of the defect, the defect injection phase can sometimes be immediately identified, or sometimes it is identified by analyzing the causes of injection. If the defect injection phase can be immediately identified, then since analysis is started with verification of the details of the documented design specifications created for that process, identifying the causes of injection is easier to do.

4.3.6   Causes of Injection

Possible causes of injection include technological root causes and root causes related to how work is performed. There is a wide variety of root causes, and they may stem from either both of these areas or just one or the other.
Furthermore, a knowledge base of accumulated defect injection causes that occurred in the past is prepared and used in order to make it easier to identify the causes of injection.

<Summary of the defect> Program exception
- When a customer entered out of limit value, then the program was aborted.

<Direct cause of the failure's occurrence>
- Threshold limit value processing for devisor 0 (zero) was not implemented

<Development history regarding the defect >
- The engineer knew the threshold limit value case that divisor was 0 (zero), but he didn't write it down to a detailed design document, because the case was too detailed to write to the document. (Then the case that divisor was 0 (zero) became "undocumented specifications".)
- It is usually performed both designing and coding by the same engineer in the organization. So, it was common that too detailed specifications were not documented.
- The engineer was switched at the end of DD (Detailed Design process) by unexpected reasons.
- New engineer coded program based on the detailed design document.
- The program was not reviewed by the previous engineer, and other engineers couldn't detect the undocumented specifications because they didn't know the specifications..
- Nobody could test the undocumented specifications.

<Specific root-cause> Undocumented specifications
- Defect injection phase: DD (Detailed Design process)
- Cause of defect injection : undocumented detailed design specifications
- Cause of defect overlook during the review: the previous engineer's absence from the coding review
- Cause of defect overlook during the testing: lack of the testing items related the defect

<1+n procedure using review>
- Scope: coding done by the new engineer
- Procedure: reviewing by the previous engineer
- Perspective: detection of any other undocumented detailed design specifications

<1+n procedure using testing>
- Scope: all undocumented detailed design specifications detected by the above 1+n procedure using review
- Procedure: testing for all the above cases
- Perspective: confirmation of normally execution of all testing items

Fig. 4-1 "Defect Root Cause Analysis and 1+n Procedure" Application Example

4.3.7   Causes of Overlook

Depending on the defect details, a defect may be detectable both during reviewing and testing, or it may not be seen as detectable during one or the other. Root causes of overlook are also analyzed from both technology and work performance angles.

Defect Root-Cause Analysis Sheet			
Reference No.:	Summary of the defect:		
Product (Project):	Version:	Defect detection date:	Registration date:
Development group:	Report: Person in charge:		
Details:			
Results expected:			
Person who detected the defect:			
Criticality: Category: Location of the defect:			
Defect introduction process			
<Cause analysis>		Technology-wise cause	Procedure-wise cause
Cause of defect introduction	High-level cause	☐Insufficient investigation of external technology	☐Essential development process skipped
		☐Insufficient investigation of internal related technology	☐Insufficient information in design specifications
		☐Insufficient programming capability	☐Violation of coding rules
		☐Insufficient coding know-how	☐Mistake in internal cooperation/handover process
		☐Insufficient information in design specifications	☐Insufficient coordination with related functions
		☐Error in design specifications	☐Insufficient development plan or insufficient plan review
		☐Insufficient interface rules	☐Others ( )
		☐Others ( )	
	Detailed description		
Cause of defect overlook	Review — High-level cause	☐No review conducted	☐Problem in review implementation method
		☐Insufficient review	☐Review not completed
		☐Omission in items to be reviewed	☐Failure to correct finding or error in finding
		☐Reviewer-related problem	☐Insufficient review plan
		☐Others ( )	☐Others ( )
	Detailed description		
	Testing — High-level cause	☐No test item defined	☐Problem in test item implementation method
		☐Error in test item	☐Test item not implemented
		☐Others ( )	☐Mistake in internal cooperation/handover process
			☐Insufficient testing plan
			☐Others ( )
	Detailed description		

Fig. 4-2 Defect Root-Cause Analysis Sheet

4.3.8 Defect Root Cause Analysis Using Defect Root Cause Analysis Sheets

The defect root cause analysis sheet in Fig. 4-2 is used in order to perform the analyses described in sections 4.4.1 through 4.4.3 above. The defect root cause analysis sheet provides examples in the "high-level cause" field, which takes accumulated defect root cause analysis results from the past and generalizes the root causes that occur with greater frequency. As a result of applying the defect root cause analysis sheet, at least 60% of root causes are seen in the examples of the high-level cause.

The user examines each single defect to consider whether or not its root cause is indicated by the items listed in the defect root cause analysis sheet's "high-level cause" items. Furthermore, the user writes the reason for the occurrence of each root cause, ranges of influence, and details in the "detailed description" field. The details are documented in the detailed description field in order to link them to the specific 1+n procedure. If the root cause is understood at the general level, it will be difficult to formulate an effective 1+n procedure. For example, if the cause of injection is "insufficient investigation of external technology", then the user writes down the specific technology that must be investigated, the investigation method, the investigation period, the person in charge of investigation, and other information in detail. This makes it possible to specifically identify the scope and details of investigation during the formulation of the 1+n procedure.

4.3.9   Criteria for Determining True Causes

The goal of defect root cause analysis is to identify a cause, in order to determine that if something specific was done, that defect would not have been injected, or it would not have been overlooked. Whether or not the range of influence and details are documented in concrete terms in the detailed description field is important. For instance, if the cause of overlook during testing is only given as "those execution conditions were not included in the test items", then that would not be concrete enough. Enough details must be provided to identify the range of influence and details regarding the reason the conditions were not included in the test items, down to a level of details such that the actual desirable test item can be derived. For instance: "Execution conditions include Condition A and Condition B. Although the range of Condition A was fully covered, Condition B was overlooked and skipped. For this reason, there were no test items regarding Condition B."

4.4   1+n Procedure Application Method

4.4.1   1+n Procedure Planning

During the 1+n procedure, the measurement details are formulated using a 1+n procedure sheet (see Fig. 4-3). If defect root cause analysis has successfully identified the precise range of influence of the root cause and other details, then the 1+n procedure is executed as is for that root cause. For instance, if the cause of overlook during review is "E design specifications were reviewed even though the C area specialist D was not present", then the 1+n procedure would be "have the C area specialist D review the E design specifications".

Next, the specific details are worked out, including that 1+n procedure's implementers, the implementation period, the number of items implemented, and the detected defect count threshold of that 1+n procedure. The forecasting of detected defect count threshold is left up to those implementing the defect root cause analysis because the possibility that same-type defects exist is greatly affected by the individual root causes and the attributes of that software, making statistical forecasting not suitable. For instance, if the aforementioned "review of E design specifications by D" is the 1+n procedure, then the possibility of latent same-type defects will greatly influenced by parts related to the C area and design details in the E design specifications to be reviewed by D, as well as the parts of the source code that match this and the difficultness of the development target software.

As with the scope of the 1+n procedure, the range of influence of the root cause is used as the range as is. Depending on the root cause, there may be cases where this range is wide. In this case, a long-term implementation is used for the 1+n procedure. Narrowing down the realistically implementable range of the 1+n procedure without justification goes against the objective of the "defect root cause analysis and 1+n procedure" technique. In actuality, there are multiple failure examples where the same-type defects that should have been detected by the 1+n procedure were removed from the scope of implementation without a valid reason, and so they occurred on the customer's side.

4.4.2   Verifying Results of Implementing 1+n Procedure

After the 1+n procedure is implemented, concerned parties gather together and verify the following, depending on the implementation results:

- If same-type defects are detected, then they verify the details of those same-type defects, validate the validity of the range and details of the 1+n procedure, and end it if there are no remaining issues.
- If a defect is detected, but it is not a same-type defect, then the probability is high that that defect was just detected by chance. They then subject that defect to analysis and implement a new "defect root cause analysis and 1+n procedure" for it.
- If no defect is detected, then they analyze the reason for this. If it is determined that the defect root cause analysis details or the 1+n procedure range or details were insufficient, then the "defect root cause analysis and 1+n procedure" is implemented again. If it is determined that there are no remaining issues, then the technique is finished.

The "defect root cause analysis and 1+n procedure" technique is implemented until there are no more remaining issues. Regardless of the number of the detected defect count, all the concerned parties gather together to verify the details of the detected defects, and consider whether or not issues remain for which the technique must be applied further. The aim is to bring together the experience and know-how of all concerned parties, and to verify whether or not any issues remain. If remaining issues are discovered, then the "defect root cause analysis and 1+n procedure" is implemented again. The entire procedure is repeatedly implemented until there are no remaining issues.

1+n Procedure Sheet		
Review procedure	Plan	Scope: Review procedure:
	Numerical target	# of items to be reviewed: # of defects to be detected: Person-hours: Period: Person in charge:
	Implementation result	
	Implementation record	# of items reviewed: # of defects detected: Person-hours: Period: Person in charge:
Testing procedure	Plan	Scope: Testing Procedure:
	Numerical target	# of test items: # of defects to be detected: erson-hours: Period: Person in charge:
	Implementation result	
	Implementation record	# of test items: # of defects detected: Person-hours: Period: Person in charge:

Fig. 4-3 1+n Procedure Sheet

4.5   Considerations

This chapter discussed the characteristics of the "defect root cause analysis and 1+n procedure", based on the previously described conclusions. In addition, it also touched upon the differences between "five whys analysis" and "defect root cause analysis".

Five whys analysis is a technique for analyzing root causes that are widely and generally applicable. Therefore, the goals of five whys analysis vary widely depending on how it is applied. As described above, in most cases, there are multiple root causes subjected to analysis, rather than just one. For this reason, unless a root cause is analyzed with a specific goal in mind, it will not be possible to arrive at the desired root cause, and multiple root causes will be analyzed. Instead of simply repeating the question "why", it is necessary to keep a specific goal in mind while working towards that goal in the analysis of root causes, or the prescribed outcome will not be achieved.

On the other hand, the "defect root cause analysis" of the "defect root cause analysis and 1+n procedure" technique is a specific root cause analysis technique that is optimized with the goal of achieving the detection of same-type defects. In order to achieve this goal, specific root causes are analyzed with a focus on the three points of "cause of injection", "cause of overlook during review", and "cause of overlook during testing" while keeping the defect injection phase of the analyzed defect in mind. This analytical framework can be provided because the "defect root cause analysis" technique organizes the structure of the defect root causes based on the precondition that the V model will be used with the goal of detecting same-type defects. Furthermore, a defect root cause analysis sheet is prepared with accumulated specific root causes from the past in order to make analysis easier. Compared to the widely applicable "five whys analysis", this technique is extremely goal-oriented.

The "1+n procedure" takes the results of this goal-oriented "defect root cause analysis", and executes measures with the specific root cause's range of influence and details as is. The technique is characterized by an avoidance of narrowing down the implementation range of the 1+n procedure without a valid reason, and by the fact that the setting of the detected defect count threshold is left up to the persons concerned.

It is said that improvements in root cause analysis capabilities contribute to the improvement of an organization's processes [4-3]. This is because the capability of precisely analyzing root causes allows the organization to precisely respond to the issues that face it. From this perspective as well, applying the "defect root cause analysis and 1+n procedure" technique and improving the "defect root cause analysis and 1+n procedure" success rate not only improves the quality of shipped software, it is also thought to contribute to improvements in the organization's processes.

4.6 Conclusion

This dissertation discusses concrete details regarding the "defect root cause analysis and 1+n procedure" technique, as well as the technique's characteristics and application method. Many development sites cannot master the use of five whys analysis in software development, and this causes a great deal of concern as it prevents effective root cause analysis. The "defect root cause analysis and 1+n procedure" technique presents one answer to this problem.

The "defect root cause analysis and 1+n procedure" technique analyzes individual specific root causes by grouping root causes into the two classifications of specific root causes and shared root causes, while narrowing down causes further into causes of injection, causes of overlook during review, and causes of overlook during testing. Since use of the V model is a precondition, once the defect injection phase is clear, identifying the root cause becomes easy. Also, past defect root cause analysis results are accumulated so that the frequently occurring root causes can be listed in the defect root cause analysis sheet, and a 1+n procedure sheet is prepared for the formulation of measures, in order to support the efficient implementation of the "defect root cause analysis and 1+n procedure". This enables the effective detection of same-type defects, based on the root causes of these defects.

It is important to tailor the method of applying five whys analysis based on the goal at hand, and with an understanding of the technique's strengths and weaknesses. "Defect root cause analysis and 1+n procedure" is a technique that is optimized with the goal of detecting same-type defects.

Chapter 5. Technologies Supporting Software Quality Accounting

5.1 Introduction

This chapter discusses the technologies that support quality accounting.

Review technology is covered first. The improvement of quality through reviewing is one of the major characteristics of quality accounting. The effectiveness of reviewing is maximized by applying quality accounting and managing the state of review implementation. This chapter describes this review technology itself.

Next, the shared mechanisms of the solutions to software quality problems worked on by a number of Japanese corporations starting in the 1970s is described. There are three mechanisms, as follows:

- Short cycle management based on data
- Quality verification from both process and product angles by an independent quality assurance department
- Release decision-making by multiple people

The practices listed above have led to implementation methods that are mostly the same, in spite of the independent quality improvement efforts by different corporations. The organization that invented NEC's quality accounting has implemented these practices, too. The meaning of this commonality is also considered below.

5.2 Review Technology

5.2.1 Positioning of Review Technology in Relation to Software Development

Review is an extremely important part of software development. As shown in Fig. 5-1, the later the process during which software defects are corrected in software development, the higher the cost of correction increases in exponential fashion [3-11]. If the cost of correcting a defect in the requirement definition stage is set at 1, then the cost of correcting that defect during design is 3 to 6 times as high, the cost during development and testing is 15 to 40 times as high, and the cost during operation balloons to 40 to 1,000 times as high [5-1]. It goes without saying that rather than working hard to detect defects during the testing stage just before operation in a production environment, extremely high cost benefits can be achieved with drastically reduced defect correction costs by detecting defects early in the design and review stages.

In spite of the fact that the effectiveness of reviewing is this high, the fact remains that not many organizations are actually implementing reviews in an effective manner. Although there are probably no examples where software is shipped without testing, examples probably do exist where software is shipped without reviewing. Possible reasons behind this include organizations not understanding how to review even if they want to, or reasoning that actually running and checking software will be quicker than thinking about how to review the software in one's head. Reviewing technology is less well-established than testing technology, and there are fewer specialized books. It is thought that since there are fewer opportunities to learn about review technology, there are many cases where organizations give up on the idea of introducing reviewing without ever effectively conducting reviews. Also, it is possible that the ability of recent technology to satisfy the requirement to actually see software running at an early stage may actually be having a counterproductive effect.

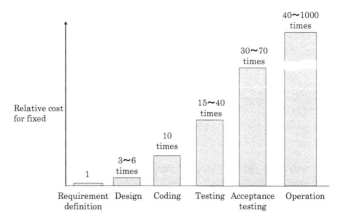

Fig. 5-1 Cost of Correcting Defects [3-11]

5.2.2 What Is Software Review?

The subjects of review during software development are not limited to design documents and programs, but also include project planning documents, requirement definition documents, test specifications, test programs, and a wide range of other items. Furthermore, not only is work output during development subject to review, sometimes review is implemented as part of testing as well. This happens in the case where, for instance, events occur at a timing such that it is difficult to reproduce them during actual operation, or when it is difficult to bring together all of the necessary software and hardware equipment, and so the review verification must be implemented at the desk. This type of review is one of the static techniques used as part of test technology. An educational effect is also sometimes expected from participation in reviews. This is the case when a young engineer participates in reviews as a part of on-the-job training. Reviews are implemented for a diverse range of goals in many different aspects of software development. This section focuses its description on the review of design documents and programs.

V&V (Verification & Validation) is an important quality assurance idea that is applied to software development. "Verification" means verifying that the work output of each development process satisfies the requirements of the previous process, and "Validation" means verifying that user needs are satisfied. Reliable implementation of V&V is the most basic foundation of software development. With V&V, verification that user needs are being satisfied is seen as a necessary part of every process. Reviews during upstream processes should be implemented with V&V in mind. In other words, the review of an upstream process based on V&V has the goal of verifying that the work output of that process satisfies the requirements of the previous process, and that the user needs that materialized up to that stage are also satisfied.

A variety of different review methods are proposed for software development (Table 5-1). There is a large number of different types, from "inspection", whereby the review procedure is decided and official records are required, to "ad hoc review", which is an informal method that is implemented on the spot. The type of review envisioned under quality accounting is closest to the "team review" type described in Table 5-1. Based on development details and necessity, however, combinations of walkthrough, pass-around, peer desk check, pair programming, ad hoc, and other review methods can also be flexibly implemented. In actuality, development sites naturally select review methods such as those listed in Table 5-1 and implement them as necessary.

A number of methods are also proposed for use in verifying reviewed work output (reading methods) (Table 5-2). Although this organization makes reviews using checklists mandatory (checklist reading), other reading methods are also applied according to development details and necessity.

A key principle of reviewing is to "hate the defect, not the person". It is important not to let one's hatred for defects lead to blaming the person who injected a defect. A review is not the place for evaluating the capabilities of those who created the object under review. A review is the place to assure quality in a constructive manner. It is also the place to share defects (failures), and to come up with ways to avoid repeating the same failures. Ensuring that all participants in a review share this type of approach is the first step towards a successful review.

5.2.3   Review Procedures

Reviews are mainly implemented from the V&V perspective so that defects can be discovered rapidly, and to consider better design methods. In order to achieve this aim, it is important to select and execute suitable review participants, review methods, and reading methods.

Figure 5-2 describes the flow of this organization's reviews. During upstream processes, the review stage is entered after a draft version of the process's work output is completed. First, the person in charge of development checks the details of the object to be reviewed, and verifies that the content is assured to be sufficient for review.

If it is not sufficient, then it is passed back. If it is ready for review, then reviewers are selected. This selection of reviewers is extremely important. Participation is not limited to just project members, but also includes the developers of software products that may be run together with the software under development, engineers who are very knowledgeable about the software area in question, related hardware engineers, people in charge of marketing, and others. If reviewers are missing here, an important defect may not be detected, and this can lead to bigger problems in subsequent processes. Actually, the author has had more than one experience where development proceeded without the necessary reviewer participating in the reviews, leading to painful situations later. For this reason, in particular during the development of software products that operate in relation with a large number, a list of parties that should verify the interface is prepared, and a check is conducted to ensure that nothing that must be verified is missing from the reviews. If the number of reviewers is large, then reviews are split into multiple theme-based reviews for the sake of efficiency. For instance, reviews can be split based on themes such as a "review of external specifications to consider the software's value as a product", or a "review focused on the interface with related software".

Before the review is actually implemented, the objects to be reviewed are distributed, and reviewers check them as much as possible in advance. In principle, reviews are conducted in a meeting format. In the case of offshore development, it is taken for granted that the reviewers will travel to the site of development for the review. Although conference calls are also used in some cases, they are limited to situations where both parties know each other well. There are also cases where an excellent reviewer is too busy to schedule time, and so the review meeting is held late at night. Regardless, it is still important to get people together and discuss things in person.

In principle, an organized review checklist is prepared, and review proceeds by applying that checklist during quality accounting. Depending on the product, in order to make the items on the review checklist easier to use for reviewing that product, expressions may be changed, items may be added, and a review checklist can be created just for that product. If the reviewers are members of the project, then the review will often involve applying the review checklist. On the other hand, if the reviewers are mainly from outside the project, then the review method will often involve having the reviewers freely indicate what they see from their standpoint.

A previously delegated recorder records items indicated during the review on the review report form (Fig. 5-3). For anything indicated that cannot be answered during the review, the creators of the objects under review investigate and report after the meeting. After the review is finished, the review report forms are organized, and defects are determined. The creators of the object that was reviewed correct it according to the review report forms, and record the correction details and dates on the review report forms. After all defects have been corrected, the revision number is incremented, and the reviewed object is issued. Those in charge of development examine the sufficiency of the review, and decide whether or not another review is required, or if it is possible to proceed to the next process. In principle, another review is held if defects continue to appear. Goals include verifying whether or not the correction of the defects injected new defects, or whether defects not discovered in the previous review may have become evident due to the correction of the defects discovered in the review. Quality analysis of the review state is implemented through upstream quality accounting (refer to section 3.3 for a description of the method of applying quality accounting to upstream processes).

Table 5-1 Various Review Methods Used in Software Development
(Created by the Author with Reference to [5-1][5-2][5-3])

	No.	Name	Details
Formal	1	Inspection	A review method designed to discover exceptions that do not meet standards or specifications. Checklists are often used. This is the most formal type of review, and requires an official record.
	2	Team Review	Review performed by a team. Not as formal as inspection; categorized as "light inspection".
	3	Walkthrough	This type of review is performed by having multiple reviewers ask questions and make comments in order to verify the details of the work under review. Whereas inspections are carried out based on previously documented formal procedures, walkthroughs are seen as lacking reproducibility because they are not proceduralized.
	4	Round-Robin Review	In this review format, all participants take turns playing the role of either chair or reviewer. This may also be referred to as a "rotating review".
	5	Peer Review	A general term for any review conducted by peers.
	6	Pair Programming	A programming method whereby two programmers share a single machine while working together. Also used as a review method, pair programming is a typical eXtreme Programming (XP) practice.
	7	Pass-Around	This review method involves the distribution (or circulation) of work to be reviewed by multiple reviewers. Electronic review (circulating an electronic file by having reviewers write comments before e-mailing the results to the next reviewer) is a type of pass-around review.
	8	Peer Desk Check	In this method, the reviewer individually reviews work, and then holds a follow-up session with the creator of the reviewed work based on a record of that review.
Casual	9	Ad Hoc Review	This informal review method simply involves asking a nearby peer for advice in order to solve a problem at hand. This is the most informal type of peer review, and is also referred to as "impromptu review".

Table 5-2 Methods of Verifying Reviewed Work (Created by the Author with Reference to [5-4])

No.	Name	Details
1	Checklist-Based Reading	A method of verifying work output using a checklist. Organized knowledge from experience based on previous defects and other such information is often used as a checklist. It can be difficult to verify every item on a checklist if there is a large number of items. The point of a checklist is to be a living document (it must be constantly reviewed so that, for instance, the items are not too abstract or too specific for the reviewer to understand them).
2	Perspective-Based Reading	With this method, the reviewer acts as a variety of different stakeholders in order to verify the work output from the standpoint or perspective of each one. Examples of perspectives include user, developer, test manager, and so on.
3	Use Case-Based Reading	Work output is verified using scenarios (use cases) created from the viewpoint of the user. This method is suitable for verifying validity.
4	Test Case-Based Reading	This method, which is derived from use case-based reading, verifies work output using test cases.

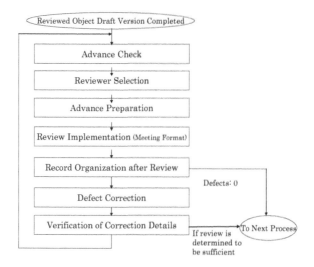

Fig. 5-2 Review Flowchart

Review report

Date							Approval	
Meetig room								
Review objectives							Rev.	
Process							Dept.	
Number of review times			Number of checked review items				Name	
Number of total review effort (person hour)			Number of detected defects					
Name of reviewer								
Number of review efforts (person hour)								

No.	Page	Function name	Pointed items	Defect	Level of importance	Revised content	Revised date

Fig. 5-3 Front of Review Report Form (Example)

It can be difficult to determine defects during a design document review. For instance, whether or not a typo is considered a defect will depend on the person conducting the review. Quality accounting defines defects in design documents (refer to Table 2-4). Depending on these definitions, an ordinary typo will not be seen as a defect, but if that typo has a high probability of causing the specifications to be misunderstood, then it will be seen as a defect. Concrete definitions are necessary so that the organization's unified determination criteria can be used to determine whether or not there are defects in design documents.

5.2.4   Review Visualization

As described in section 2.5.1, since software includes attributes that cannot be seen, methods must be worked out to visualize these attributes during review.

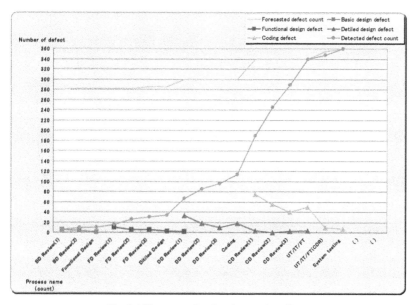

Fig. 5-4 Upstream Quality Accounting Chart

Quality accounting requires visualization based on the ideas of defect injection and detection (refer to section 3.3.2 for a description of defect injection and detection). During upstream quality accounting, the detected defects are classified into defect injection phases, and the detection trends are plotted in a time series graph (Fig. 5-4). In the quality accounting technique, review analysis occurs during the defect analysis for each injection phase (refer to section 3.4.3). Unless the trend in defects detected by each review is at least moving downward for the process, it is not judged to have been completed. If the trend in defects increases the more reviews are conducted, this is seen as evidence that defects are still hidden, and reviews are continued. In this case, the viewpoint from which reviews are seen to be insufficient is analyzed, and measures are taken such as having engineers knowledgeable in that viewpoint participate in reviews. Also, since the defects are graphed, it is possible to see abnormal situations such as with a single glance, such as when upstream defects in basic design or other areas are being detected in subsequent processes. If defects from upstream processes continue to be detected, then whether or not it is necessary to return to that process in order to head off the source of the defects and review again is considered.

5.2.5   Effects of Review

The goal of upstream quality accounting is to rapidly detect any defects injected during a certain process before the next process starts. The target upstream defect detection rate for quality accounting is 80%. This means that 20% of the defects injected during that process should still remain at the start of the testing process. Organizations that have correctly applied quality accounting will achieve an upstream defect detection rate of 80%.

Reviews greatly improve software quality. The idea that reviews take a long time and testing is faster is a major mistake. Reviews and tests both have their strengths and weaknesses (refer to Table 5-3). Since testing involves actual operation of the product, it requires a large amount of time as well as personnel, facilities, and expenses. Reviewing, on the other hand, can detect many times the number of defects detected during the same amount of time spent testing, simply by gathering together engineers with the appropriate skills for several hours. The earlier reviews are conducted, the higher the cost benefit. Also, reviews can even detect defects that are difficult to detect by actual operation of the software. Since reviews are only verifications at the desk, however, they cannot be used for final verifications. Since tests involve actual operation of the software, even if there are differences in ideas between engineers, this still does not lead to things being overlooked. The relationship between the software and the hardware that is operated at the same time can also be verified.

If reviews are conducted based on an understanding of their strengths and weaknesses, they should work to greatly improve the quality of software.

5.2.6   Summary

The review is a powerful tool for improving the quality of software. Unfortunately, at present it is a tool that is not being used very well. As was mentioned in this section, there are fewer Japanese books on review technology than there are on test technology, and so reviews are an area of technology that should be aggressively pursued in the future. When compared to Europe and the US, Japanese software development focuses more on the importance of reviews, and there are multiple examples of how reviews were implemented with successful results. Reviews conducted at actual development sites should be brought together in order to pursue the establishment of review techniques that are even more concrete and practical.

Table 5-3 Characteristics of Reviewing and Testing

		Reviewing	Testing
Advantages		· Can be implemented at low cost · Good and bad parts of program structure can be checked · Can detect redundant or wasteful logic · Can verify that development matches contractual terms	· Can verify actual processing results · Can verify along with related hardware/software · Nothing overlooked due to misunderstandings, since verification uses actual equipment · Can detect issues missed in design considerations
Disadvantages		· Bad at detecting missing functions that reviewers are unaware of · Risk of overlooked problems exists; not suited for use as a method of final verification	· Difficult to create test conditions and environments · Processing results might come out correctly in spite of mistakes (in cases such as when something is overlooked in default setting ranges)

5.3   Mechanisms for Ensuring Quality

This section described mechanisms shared by a number of Japanese corporations in the solutions they have been working on for software quality problems since the 1970s [3-1][3-2][3-3][3-4]. The mechanisms described in this section have converged on essentially the same implementation method, in spite of the fact that they started out as efforts to improve quality by different corporations. The organization that invented NEC's quality accounting has also implemented the same mechanism.

5.3.1   Short Cycle Management Based on Data

Data-based management is a shared mechanism that is being used by all Japanese corporations. This is a foundational idea in CMMI as well, and is described in a number of process areas.

Data-based management is taken one step further here with management based on data in short cycles (at least weekly). Organizations that are successful in improving quality are all achieving a rapid understanding of problems soon after they occur by implementing management based on short data cycles. With the management method of receiving reports after problems are solved, it is only possible to verify problem resolution results. By rapidly understanding problems after they occur, with all concerned parties in agreement while precisely ascertaining the true cause of the problems and implementing countermeasures, and verifying the on-site state using data to come to conclusions, it is possible for concerned parties to bring together and use their different experiences and know-how.

Furthermore, if the management implementation method is face-to-face, communication is improved further, and it becomes easier to take actions that are practical and effective, rather than just formal.

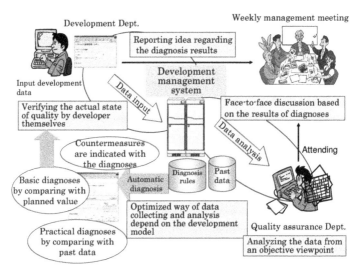

Fig. 5-5 Efficient Development Management
through Development Management Systems

An actual example of collection and analytical use from the organization that invented quality accounting is presented here (refer to Fig. 5-5). The organization that invented quality accounting developed and is running its own development management system for the sake of data collection and analysis. Management meetings are held at the same time and on the same day weekly, and the date and time deadlines for data input are also set based on the day of the week. The developers input the development results for that week in a development management system, when has a function that automatically diagnoses them. This automatic diagnosis function checks for mistakes in data input and other areas, and diagnoses the state of basic quality by following automatic diagnosis rules set using planned values and comparisons with accumulated data from the past. Based on this, the developer can use the inputted data to check basic items. These basic items include checking the state of review and test implementation, defect detection data, and other information to diagnose whether or not reviewing or testing is insufficient, and to verify the actual state of quality as compared to the plan. The developer considers the results of diagnosis, and attends management meetings after formulating countermeasures as necessary. The same data is also used by the quality assurance department to implement quality analyses. Since the quality assurance department attends each weekly management meeting, it can grasp the state of development in a timely fashion. Quality analysis is implemented while adding the information up to the previous management meeting, and the results are taken to the next management meeting. The development and quality assurance departments bring together each individual analysis result and measure, and discuss and implement ideal measures.

On principle, the organization that invented quality accounting holds face-to-face management meetings. This is because based on past experience, face-to-face meetings make it easier to precisely grasp the problems of the development site.

5.3.2   Verifying Quality from Both Process and Product Angles Using Independent
         Quality Assurance Departments

One representative example of how a number of Japanese corporations arrived at the same implementation method is the existence of a quality assurance department that is independent from the development department [5-5]. Although the functions performed by these quality assurance departments differ somewhat, they all grasp the state of progress of each process through data analysis during development at the development site from an objective viewpoint, while verifying the quality of each process's work output, and using some method of actually testing and evaluating the final work output. No matter how excellent a developer is, it is difficult to maintain an objective viewpoint throughout the course of development. The function of verifying quality through the use of an independent department separate from the development department is a mandatory part of the quality assurance mechanism. Also, in the same way as development requires development technology, quality verification also requires technology for verifying quality. To this end, quality specialists are also necessary.

When the situation is examined globally, almost all quality assurance departments independent from development departments are teams that specialize in testing. Quality assurance is undertaken by these teams as a part of testing. For instance, test teams such as those who implement system tests are a typical example. The closest thing to the type of quality assurance departments that exists in Japan is IV&V (Independent Verification & Validation) [2-12]. As the name indicates, this is an organization that implements V&V independently from the development department. With the definition of IV&V, however, V&V is often implemented by a provider that differs from the provider that received the order for the development activities, and the IV&V method is often decided based on development examples, which is different from the way a Japan corporation maintains a quality assurance department as a fixed organization. Also, with Japanese-style quality assurance departments, the development department itself implements V&V, and the quality assurance department also implements quality assurance activities, so this is also fundamentally different from IV&V. Furthermore, in the case of IV&V, it is difficult to feed the results of IV&V back for use in process revision. The benefits of maintaining a quality assurance department as a fixed organization include the accumulation of know-how and the ability to make systematic improvements based on this know-how. This makes it easier to collect examples of success and failure as an organization, and to concentrate this information in one location so that it is easy to reflect feedback on processes.

Quality must be verified from both process and product quality angles. This is also a principle of quality management (refer to section 2.4.2 in chapter 2). The things that can be understood separately from process quality or product quality are limited. Process quality verification ensures that the tasks that should be executed for each process have been completed reliably, and product quality verification ensures that the completed work output reliably satisfies the predetermined requirements. The overall status can only be grasped reliably by combining both forms of quality verification (see Fig. 5-6).

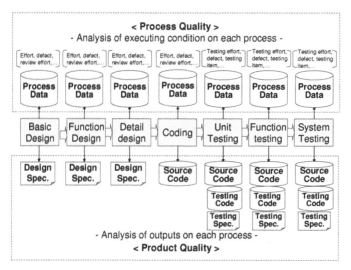

Fig. 5-6 Quality Assurance Combining Both Process Quality and Product Quality
Using a Quality Assurance Department

5.3.3　Release Decision-Making by Multiple People

Release decision-making by multiple people is an implementation method shared by
Japanese corporations [5-5]. With release decision-making being conducted by the
person in charge of a development project alone, that developer's judgment tends to be
swayed by the fact that he has responsibility for the project. By having those outside the
project's command structure also be involved in release decision-making, it becomes
possible to conduct release decision-making from the customer's perspective. A
representative example of a decider outside the command structure is the person in
charge of the quality assurance department. The person in charge of the quality
assurance department understands the results of the process and product quality
verification performed by that organization, as well as the history of development. Also,
since he possesses data for other development projects too, including data from after
shipment, he can make more objective decisions while considering the causal
relationships before and after shipment.

Release decision-making standards should be set clearly in advance, and should all be
in the form of standards that allow for decision based on numerical values, if possible.
Furthermore, release decision-making standards must include standards that allow for

91

the precise determination of the completion of testing. Product evaluation by a quality assurance department is also one more type of important information that must be used for making the decision. In the case of quality accounting, the exit criteria in software testing adopts determination results based on the three techniques of "defect trend assessment", "defect root cause analysis and 1+n procedure", and "defect convergence determination".

Since multiple people are involved in release decision-making, it is necessary to clarify the method for deciding what to do if the determination result is split. In this case, the determination result of the person in charge of the quality assurance department should be adopted. This is to prevent the adoption of a determination by the person in charge of the development department, which could be swayed by the interests of the developers. Also, it is important to prepare a method to handle the case from a business standpoint were the determination is that the product is not ready for release. At the organization that invented quality accounting, if the person in charge of business approves, the scope of shipment can be limited, or special shipments can occur with conditions attached, based on a so-called "waiver" method. Even in this case, however, release decision-making is implemented until the product passes, and there is a mechanism to certify it for the first time as an officially shipped product after it passes.

The implementation of release decision-making by multiple people makes it possible to always use the same fair release decision-making standards. This fact has a major effect on engineers, because software under development and final work output software cannot be shipped unless it meets predetermined standards. If the standards are not satisfied, then rejection is the decision regarding the release-decision making. When they experience this for themselves, this motivates engineers to take the initiative for themselves and consider quality assurance, resulting in a self-directed process improvement cycle.

5.4   Conclusion

This chapter described the review technology that supports quality accounting, as well as the practices of a number of Japanese corporations.

At the organization that invented quality accounting, at the same time as quality accounting was being invented, quality assurance mechanisms for eliciting the effects of quality accounting were also being continuously developed. These mechanisms eventually converged with the quality assurance mechanisms invented independently by a number of different Japanese corporations. It is due to this fact that it became evident that there is now a practice for achieving quality improvement that could even be referred to as an "orthodox method". This method is comprised of three elements: short cycle management based on data, quality verification from both process and product angles by an independent quality assurance department, and release decision-making by multiple people.

At the organization that invented quality accounting, in order to resolve issues that occur in the application of quality accounting, new techniques such as design and test techniques have been introduced and continuously improved. Review technology is an important part of these techniques. Also, the construction of quality assurance mechanisms that can build in quality throughout the entire software process is indispensable for quality assurance. The three mechanisms described above are important elements of this.

The quality accounting technique is a quality management technique, and the scope over which quality accounting can be effective by itself is limited. Quality accounting plays a role in guiding improvements in quality. The application of quality accounting clarifies problem points in software development, and can be used to find clues in the analysis of their causes. The technologies and mechanisms for eliciting the effects of the quality accounting that is constructed as a result are indispensable for improving quality.

Chapter 6. Software Factory

6.1 Introduction

The consolidation of development technology, management technology, development environments, and other elements is an essential part of efficient software development. The organization that invented quality accounting has been working on developing software development environments and technology since the 1970s. In recent years, as development tools with easy-to-use capabilities have spread, it has become important to build optimal development environments by combining these develop tools and technologies. This chapter discusses these efforts.

6.2 History of the Software Factory

Since the scale of software grew rapidly in the 1970s, that was a period during which a variety of different problems also arose as a result. In particular, the increasing cost of dealing with software defects grew severe, and software quality problems became management issues. This is the situation so-called "Software Crisis". In order to respond to this Software Crisis, NEC started SWQC in 1981 [3-6]. SWQC (SoftWare Quality Control) is a comprehensive set of software quality management activities, and the first attempt in the world to implement software quality management activities throughout an entire company. This effort was based on the idea that "software should be built using methods similar to engineering or production, rather than crafting or home manufacturing" (Dr. Yukio Mizuno, Ph.D., former senior executive vice president of NEC). The philosophy of SWQC is to "pursue quality first; productivity can come later", with the goal of "achieving software that the user will be glad to purchase, and which will contribute to the advancement of society". SWQC activities include both a top-down approach starting with upper management, and a bottom-up approach starting with a focus on small group activities. At present, SWQC is being continued in an SWQC community format, as a way for software developers to interact by going beyond the corporate structure.

A wide range of other software development research efforts were also pursued in addition to the start of SWQC activities. The Software Factory is one of these efforts.

The statement "rather than referring to a software 'production factory' as simply a building with a row of desks where 'craftsmen' work, I would like to see this act as a detonator for starting the development of a modern, highly productive factory that accumulates the 'know-how' necessary to produce high-quality products" (by professor emeritus Dr. Shigeichi Moriguchi, Ph.D., at the University of Tokyo) was recorded at a regular study group attended by experts. This was the spark that started the efforts leading to the Software Factory.

Fig. 6-1 shows the history of the evolution of the Software Factory at the organization that invented quality accounting. Along with the growth of SWQC activities throughout the entire company, in the 1980s development technologies such as design, review, and test technologies were consolidated, as well as quality accounting and other management technologies, through the development of tools. All of this occurred during the era in which mainframe computers were the norm.

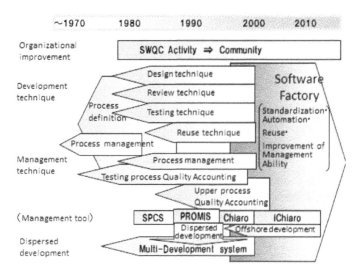

Fig. 6-1 Evolution of the Software Factory

In the 1990s, a paradigm shift referred to as "neodama" occurred. This Japanese acronym stands for "network, open, downsizing, and multimedia", and takes the first Japanese syllable for each of these words. Tools that ran on high-performance PCs were released one after another, and software development was strongly influenced by this trend, in both good and bad ways. Since created software could be executed immediately, mistaken ideas such as "detailed design is not necessary" and "unit testing is not necessary" spread. Although during the mainframe era, restrictions on time spent using expensive mainframes were strict, and so it was necessary to verify as much as possible at the desk, once inexpensive execution environments became ubiquitous in the open era, the emphasis shifted to the use of those execution environments.

In the 2000s, adverse effects started to occur due to the influence of the open era. Since now there were software development environments optimized for each product, it became difficult to execute organized engineering measures. For instance, in order to install a unified tool, it became necessary to install separate development tools for each product's software development environment, and this required the application of a large amount of effort and time. In 2004, the organization that invented quality accounting was informed when it achieved CMMI level 5 verification that it had a "weak point in the organized consideration of engineering", and so it took this opportunity to start considering construction of the Software Factory. The author contributed to the establishment of the Software Factory concept and basic design as the leader of these considerations. Since the start of construction of the Software Factory, the author has continued to participate in an assistant leader capacity.

6.3 Construction Philosophy

The software development environment of a famous global software corporation was benchmarked during the construction of the Software Factory. The Software Factory was then modeled based on these results, as shown in Table 6-1. Based on the arrangement of functions that the Software Factory should possess, four types were made, including [A] Centered model, [B] Nearly Centered model, [C] Shared model, and [D] Dispersed model. Of these, the most advanced model is [A] Centered model. Software corporations with this model have engineers dispersed throughout the world log into one physical Software Factory to develop. This made it realistic to develop something in the US one day, and continue development in Europe the next day. Development assets were all concentrated in a single Software Factory location, and this made it extremely efficient to understand the state of development, manage development assets, switch between tools, and so on.

Table 6-1 Modeling of The Software Factory

	[A] Centered model	[B] Nearly Centered model	[C] Shared model	[D] Dispersed model
Forma-tion	One center factory	One center factory and multiple local factories	One center factory and multiple local factories	Multiple center factories and local factories
Feature	•All functions are provided in center factory. •All engineers develop software at the center factory	•All functions are provided in center factory. •A part of testing is executed at local factories	•Management functions are provided in center factory. •Others are shared by center and local factories.	•All functions are provided in center factories or local factories.

At the time, the organization that invented quality accounting was a [D] Dispersed model. It would run software development environments for each product, and development assets where managed either at a center factory or a local factory, or both. Since development tools were selected based on the attributes of each product, they were not unified when viewed at the organizational level. Actually, however, during the mainframe era of the 1980s, the organization that invented quality accounting was an [A] Centered model Software Factory. Since owning a separate expensive mainframe for each product was a practical impossibility, the only choice was to keep things centered. As the organization switched to open systems, however, development environments, development languages, execution environments, supported platforms, and so on gradually began to diverge for each product, and separate optimization progressed along with the advancement of offshore development and other forms of distributed development, until the organization changed to the [D] Dispersed model.

Based on the results of this investigation, the organization that invented quality accounting decided to select the Software Factory's [B] Nearly Centered model. The [B] Nearly Centered model concentrates basic functions in a center factory, and can only conduct partial testing at distributed development bases. Based on considerations of the attributes of middle software development products for use in IT products, testing on a wide variety of actual storage and network equipment is necessary, and it became impossible on a practical level to concentrate all of this testing in the center due to the distributed development system including offshore development.

6.4 Aims of the Software Factory

The Software Factory is a system that integrates software development methodologies, tools, and environments. The goal of the Software Factory is a major improvement in software development quality and productivity. The aims behind achieving the goals of the Software Factory are shown in Table 6-2. The four aims are standardization, automation, reuse, and improvement of management ability. Standardization, automation, and reuse are pursued in this order.

Table 6-2 Aim of The Software Factory

Aim	content	item
Standardization	Centralized and unified process, methodology and tools	• Standardization of process, environment and tools • Consolidation of supported works
Automation	Automation in all software development scenarios	• Automation of process, environment and tools • Daily build and testing
Reuse	Reuse of architectures, codes, and documents	• Reuse of architecture, design and code • Reuse of structured document
Improvement of Management ability	"Real-timeness", improved data accuracy, corporate management system collaboration	• Automated static verification • Prevention of security violation • Intellectual property management

The aims of the Software Factory are described below.

(1) Standardization

Ultimate standardization is pursued through the advancement of standardization in every development scenario. This standardization procedure seeks to consolidate work that all projects have in common. For instance, specialized engineering groups consolidate and execute such tasks as standardizing processes and tools, as well as updating engineering technology, while operational groups consolidate and execute such tasks as supplementary development, including work output backup. This makes it possible to maintain the latest software development environment at a minimal cost. Users of the Software Factory can concentrate on software development, which is their original mission.

By having a specialized group handle supplementary development work, it is expected that such work can be made more efficient and advanced. This is because the use of specialized groups naturally promotes streamlining and advancement within each group as members work to preserve their positions while improving their work.

(2) Automation

Automation is promoted in every part of software development. In addition to automatic building and automatic testing, the latest tools are used to conduct automatic checks, which dramatically improves both quality and productivity. The discussion and introduction of new tools can be difficult unless discussion occurs within groups specializing in engineering. If a developer attempts to do this by himself during a busy work period, then it will inevitably cause work to come to a halt.

(3) Reuse

There are future plans to focus on reuse as an important area. Complicated and invisible software attributes (refer to section 2.5 in chapter 2) are extremely difficult to reuse.

Current efforts focus on promoting realistic reuse during each stage of software development. Although the reuse of source code is central to the current stage, in the future, reuse at the architecture and design level will be pursued. This organization applies UML as a standard, and is considering promoting reused based on UML.

(4) Improvement of management ability

Application of the Software Factory is useful for enabling the maximum use of data that can be collected, as well as for management. For instance, progress management based on incremental work output as it is checked in on a daily basis, and static validation tools that run in the middle of the night to verify the details of work output, are used to implement a system whereby management is possible based on actual objects, rather than just relying on reports from the developer. The prevention of information leaks and intellectual property management are also important. The Software Factory uses features such as access control and intellectual property infringement checks to prevent problems before they occur.

For software development to succeed, the quality and management of human resources are much more important factors than tools and technologies [2-14]. Therefore, improvements in management capabilities are extremely important.

6.5   Overview and Effects of the Software Factory

An overview of the Software Factory is provided in Fig. 6-2. The Software Factory provides software developers with a development environment in a cloud format. All functions are consolidated in a center factory, and development assets are managed in an integrated manner. Since the center factory is constructed at a data center, it runs 24/7. Development assets are automatically backed up each night, and stored at remote data centers. The Software Factory is constructed on an intranet with access control. A single VM (Virtual Machine) is assigned to each project. The only engineers with access to this VM are the ones registered as project members for that project. The Software Factory is run by a specialized operational team. This operational team is also in charge of updating all of the software used in the Software Factory, and always maintains software in the most recent state. From the user's perspective, the Software Factory is a development environment that is guaranteed to always be in an optimal state.

The effectiveness of the Software Factory is shown in Table 6-3. The Software Factory offers major benefits, not only at the site of development, but from a management viewpoint as well. Not only are investments in development environments optimized, measures at the management level are also quickly implemented. Since Software Factories in Japan are also usable from international bases, they can also be applied easily towards distributed development at the global level.

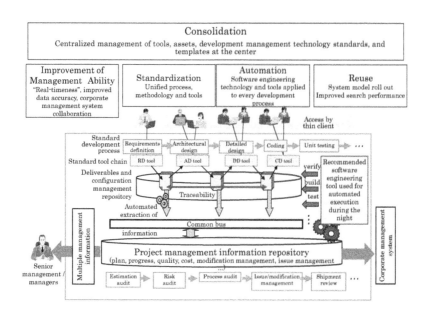

Fig. 6-2 Concept Model of the Software Factory

Table 6-3 Merits and benefits of the Software Factory

	Management viewpoint	Engineer's viewpoint
Cost	◦ Can optimize entire development investment (costs of equipment, training, etc). ◦ Effective for energy-saving and CO2 emissions limits.	◦ Can acquire better development methodologies and environments at lower costs. *The acquisition is easy and quick.
Management and control	◦ Can cascade instructions and measures immediately and ensure they are followed thoroughly. ◦ Can take measures at a best timing and have them followed immediately.	◦ Can improve management accuracy by giving importance to the "actual spot" and the "actual object". ◦ Can analyze issues and draw up improvement plans based on standardized metrics.
Human resource	◦ Promotes organizational-level acquisition of know-how (to terminate reliance on individual skills) ◦ Can use resources flexibly by the improvement in human resource fluidity as a result of the above.	◦ Can focus on the development work (including communication, design and improvement activities). ◦ Can improve individual skills through experience of advanced and global de facto development environment.

6.6 Improvements in Quality and Productivity Due to the Software Factory

This section describes Software Factory functions that are already implemented at the current time. The functions implemented currently are centered on source programs, and mainly include streamlining and management enhancement capabilities.

Functions for promoting efficient projects are described below, along with their effects.

(1) Starting a new project in two days

When a new project is started, all that is necessary to prepare that project's development environment is to provide information such as the project name and project user roster. A project can be started two days from the submission of this project information. Before the Software Factory existed, it would have been necessary to prepare a development server for this project, install tools such as configuration management software, register project members with access, and so on. These tasks would have taken at least two weeks before the project could start.

(2) Integrated access management

Access management is extremely important when it comes to the maintenance of development assets during development. It is necessary to ensure that only people with access privileges can actually access the project's development assets. Also, it is possible to narrowly define access scopes for project members, depending on their roles. For instance, it is possible to set up access so that the project leader can access all project data, but offshore development members can only access the parts related to offshore development.

(3) Static validation of periodic work output

With the Software Factory static validation of source programs is executed every night, and the results of this can be referenced the next morning. In addition to daily increments to source programs, it is also possible to check from the following viewpoints on a daily basis.

- Size of each source file, including numbers of comment lines, executable lines, and blank lines, as well as the appropriateness of the ratios between these values
- Appropriateness of complexity, nesting depth, and other aspects based on numerical values
- Existence of areas suspected to be defects
- Existence of cloned code

102

The viewpoints listed above are attributes related to source program maintainability, not defects. For instance, even if a program is deeply nested, this does not necessarily mean that it will have execution problems. However, when one considers program maintenance from a long-term perspective, if a program is deeply nested, modifying it will carry a higher risk of defect injection. These problems cannot be corrected, even if they are discovered after testing is complete. It is during coding that these issues can be resolved by modifying the code. That is why the environment with its nightly execution of static validation checks are thought to contribute to maintainability.

It is also important to make adjustments so that each individual tool's execution results can be used immediately at the site of software development. For instance, if the code check tool is simply executed, thousands of messages will be listed, from items that are almost certainly defects down to simple notifications, in numbers too large for a human to process them all. Since engineers need to investigate all messages one item at a time, from important messages to unnecessary messages, so this takes an extremely long time and is inefficient. With the tool implemented in the Software Factory, messages that are seen as needing modification can be narrowed down in the execution results, so the engineer only needs to respond to messages that have been carefully selected. Also, since the tools are adjusted so that there are no duplicate results between them, this also assists the engineer in efficiently conducting work.

Furthermore, periodic static validation also has effects from the management perspective. Static validation of work output makes it possible to grasp actual work output in real time. This makes it possible to identify and create countermeasures for work output with problems in maintainability during development, and to prevent the occurrence of problems in advance such as maintenance issues after shipment and problems during modification. Since before there was the Software Factory, it was not possible to verify the quality of work output until the final work output is shipped, it was difficult to implement countermeasures even if problems were discovered.

(4) Automatic building and testing

The Software Factory includes automatic building and testing functions. For this reason, if both build and test conditions are registered, daily building and testing can be implemented. Before the Software Factory, unless automatic building and testing functions were prepared on one's own, builds used to be major tasks. Gathering and building the latest files would take around half a day. Since building was a manual task, it was easy to make mistakes, but these mistakes would generally only be discovered after tests were executed. For this reason, time-consuming backtracking was often required.

(5) Advancement and refinement of management

The various problems that can occur during project implementation are managed through the issuance of tickets. In addition to failures during testing, there are also specification change proposals, project implementation adjustment items, and various other types of tickets. Of these, defects are used as defect management information. The quality analysis of quality accounting also uses this information. The benefits to this system that did not exist before stem from the fact that tickets are linked to configuration management information. The details before and after each defect is corrected can be verified while referencing the source program. For this reason, in cases such as when defects increase suddenly during testing or do not stop occurring, it is possible to grasp the trend in defects by verifying the details of specific defects, one defect at a time. Before the Software Factory, this is information that would not have been available unless time was spent in investigation.

Since action items are also managed as tickets, it is possible to grasp the current remaining action items, persons in charge, and progress state in real time. If there is an engineer or other factor acting as a bottleneck, then it is possible to change the person in charge with the tool by using tickets. This is information that was not available outside the weekly project management meeting in the era before the Software Factory was created.

6.7   Conclusion

This chapter described the Software Factory's positioning, overview, and effectiveness. The Software Factory combines tools and technologies that have already existed in the world in order to provide major improvements in efficiency as a whole. These efforts to combine the benefits of each individual tool, and to ensure that they function well as a whole, are extremely advantageous during a software development project. The most important advantage is actually the psychological benefit of freeing engineers from the various hassles involved in software development. The biggest aim of the Software Factory is allowing engineers to focus on their original mission, which is software development.

The Software Factory is an important measure for resolving the difficulties surrounding implementation, including the meticulous and accurate development tasks and work output required during software development. Even if they attempt to carefully verify this type of meticulousness and accuracy, people still tend to overlook things as this is an area that they find difficult. Resolving this problem with a thorough mechanism is an important part of implementing high-quality software development.

The management benefits of the Software Factory are also no less important. Although there are still many functions that are planned for future implementation in the Software Factory, even though work on the system is not yet complete, cost-saving benefits are already being seen. The system is already being applied to offshore development, and its benefits in risk management are major. The Software Factory prepares backup sites as a countermeasure should disaster strike, and since it is operated at data centers, it is already robust with respect to disasters from the start. The Software Factory is currently being deployed throughout NEC as a company-wide measure.

Chapter 7. Actual Cases of Quality Improvements Made through Application of Software Quality Accounting

7.1 Introduction

This chapter introduces three examples of how quality improvements were actually achieved through the application of software quality accounting. The first example is the organization that invented quality accounting (referred to as "Organization A" below). Organization A invented the technique of quality accounting, constructed the current technique, and applied it in order to achieve improvements in quality. In the second example, an organization that applied quality accounting and yet still suffered from quality problems (referred to as "Organization B" below) revised its previous quality accounting application method as well as its entire software development mechanism and achieved effects after application. The third example describes quality improvements in offshore development conducted in China. Offshore development is software development that occurs overseas. In this example of the application of quality accounting and the revision of the mechanism for overall software development at an offshore development base (referred to as "Organization C" below), both quality and productivity are improved. These improvement examples show that the strict application of quality accounting and comprehensive efforts regarding the entire software process surrounding quality accounting are effective means of achieving high-quality software development.

In quality improvement examples for both Organization A and Organization B, the absolute values of post-release defect counts are used as indices for determining quality. The reasons post-release defect counts are not normalized based on development scale or other factors are that 1) from the customer's perspective, the post-release defect count itself as seen from the customer is an important aspect indicating quality, 2) the post-release defect count of the general-purpose software product is greatly influenced by the number of customers and the harshness of the environments used by the customers, and is not proportionally related to the scale of development, and 3) at shipment, the scale of development has no bearing on the condition of shipment from the customer's perspective. Therefore, the assumption is that normalization is not required. Based on this assumption, the absolute value of the post-release defect count is used to set the organization's quality improvement target, which is then used in threshold management at both Organization A and Organization B.

7.2 Organization A Quality Improvement Example

Organization A is the organization that invented the software quality accounting technique. By inventing and applying quality accounting, Organization A achieved the remarkable result of reducing the annual post-release defect counts to 1/20th of what they used to be over 20 years ago. Since then, the environment surrounding Organization A's software business has experienced several paradigm shifts, including a switch from mainframes to open systems, the emergence of open source software (OSS), the advancement of offshore development, and others. During that time, Organization A has continued quality improvement activities in order to respond to these changes, and has maintained this level of post-release defect counts.

This section describes the case of Organization A, including its invention of software quality accounting, from the 1980s up to the present day. Ever since being assigned to work in Organization A's quality assurance department, the author has participated in the construction and application of software quality accounting, and has played a central role in contributing to Organization A's quality improvement activities.

7.2.1 Organization A Quality Improvement Activities

As shown in the history of quality accounting construction in Fig. 7-1, quality accounting passed through three development stages before arriving at its current form. The three stages of the development of quality accounting and Organization A's efforts are described below.

(1) First stage: quality improvement by detecting defects through intensive testing

Organization A was inspired to invent software quality accounting as a means of solving its own quality problems. Since Organization A's post-release defect count was high at the time, it was caught in a downward spiral that caused its development to fall behind schedule as it struggled to resolve all of its defects. Developers were growing exhausted by all the work involved in pursuing solutions, and it became imperative that some way be found to resolve the quality problems. To this end, Organization A's first efforts along these lines were to be the first stage, or "quality improvement by detecting defects through intensive testing" (see Fig. 7-1). The idea was to strengthen testing in order to detect as many defects as possible, thereby reducing the number of post-release defects. The "testing quality accounting" technique was invented during this first stage of quality accounting construction, and defect detection during testing processes was managed using thresholds. Organization A worked to establish technologies including the regression-based defect count forecast model used to set defect count thresholds, and the defect convergence determination used to determine when testing should end. The organization also embarked on a program of standardization, splitting into discussion groups based on topics such as management technology, design technology, testing process technology, and review technology, engaging in proactive efforts aimed at standardizing technology. The first versions of the resulting standards were mostly issued between 1986 and 1989, or from the end of the first stage to the year the second stage was launched (see Fig. 7-1).

Fig. 7-2 shows the trend of Organization A's post-release defect count, using relative values with 1985's post-release defect count set as 100. The three stages of the construction of quality accounting are labeled at the bottom of the graph, with the first stage corresponding to the period from 1985 to 1988. Due to the activities conducted during this first stage, by 1988 the post-release defect count was approximately half of what it was in 1985.

(2) Second stage: quality improvement by early defect detection within upstream processes

Although the detection of defects during testing in the first stage did produce quality improvement results, strengthening testing during the final process tended to lead to shipment schedule delays. This led to a gradual shift of focus towards improving quality starting with upstream processes, and the second stage, which was "quality improvement by early defect detection within upstream processes" (see Fig. 7-1). During the second stage, Organization A strengthened defect detection through reviews, and invented "upstream quality accounting" to detect defects during review using threshold management. In addition, the organization worked to establish quality decision tables for use in determining the state of quality based on the relationship between reviews and defect detection, and defect trend assessment for analyzing defect detection trends. The main index used to detect defects during reviews is the upstream defect detection rate. The upstream defect detection rate is the ratio of defects discovered during reviews over the total number of pre-release defects. During the second stage, which corresponded to the period from 1989 to 1995, the post-release defect count dropped even further, and Organization A's post-release defect count fell to 1/20th of the level in 1985 (see Fig. 7-2). The upstream defect detection rate also continued to improve during the second stage, exceeding 80% (see Fig. 7-3). Organization A has since continued to maintain the same standard of post-release defect counts, and upstream defect detection rates greater than 80%.

(3) Third stage: feedback to the development process though defect root cause analysis

The organization is currently in the third stage, "feedback to the development process though defect root cause analysis". This is based on the process-oriented idea that "good software is created through good processes". Defect root cause analysis is used to analyze root causes, and feedback to the development processes is used in an effort to maintain good processes through constant revision. As a result of these efforts, Organization A was verified as having achieved CMMI Level 5 in 2004.

Fig. 7-4 shows the CMMI Level and the upstream defect detection rate. Although the Level 5 upstream defect detection rate requirement is 65%, Organization A's upstream defect detection rate is greater than 80%. This effect is due to software quality accounting in general, and upstream quality accounting in particular.

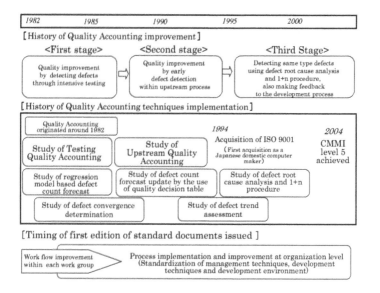

Fig. 7-1 Construction of Quality Accounting

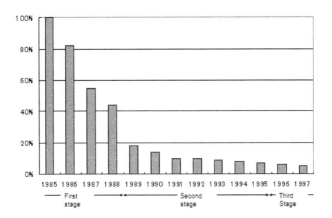

Fig. 7-2 Trend chart showing decrease in post-release defect count
(This chart shows the relative ratio against the post-release defect count in 1985)

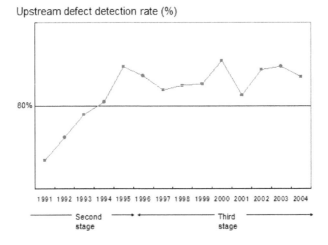

Fig. 7-3 Trend chart showing the improvement of upstream defect detection rate

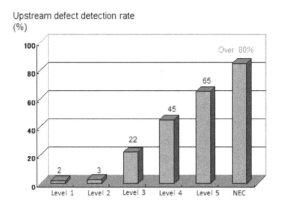

Fig. 7-4 Upstream defect detection rate and CMMI level

(Data source of the data corresponding to level 1 to level 5: NIKKEI Computer (Published 2001.7.30.))

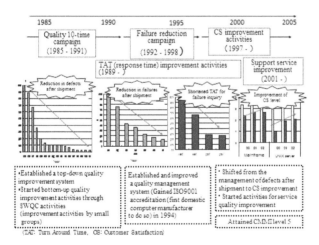

Fig. 7-5 Efforts for Improving Software Quality and Productivity at Organization A

Up to the present, Organization A has maintained a level of post-release defect counts that is 1/20th that of the 1985 level. In addition to this reduction in the post-release defect count, the organization has also implemented more than 20 years of improvement activities, including reduced problems and increased customer satisfaction levels (see Fig. 7-5). Organization A was originally a mainframe operating system developer, but as the business environment shifted towards open systems, IT middle software took over as its main development products, and in response to the emergence of open-source software, it moved towards support for service businesses using offshore development and other changing development environments, all the while maintaining a low level of post-release defect counts. The organization's low post-release defect count is one of its strong points, and it has a quality-oriented software engineering culture. This is an awareness that is shared from the top on down to developers working on-site.

7.2.2   Considerations

This section considers the reasons Organization A was able to achieve the aforementioned effects.

It is thought that in addition to the invention and application of software quality accounting, streamlining of the overall software processes through development technology standardization and other means as well as the effects of the organization-wide promotion of quality improvements also were behind the reduction of post-release defect counts to 1/20th and the achievement of upstream defect detection rates of 80%. Quality accounting can be said to have acted as a powerful driving force behind the realization of these improvements, and at least approximately 50% of the effects are seen as direct results of quality accounting itself, for the following reasons:

- One of the strengths of quality accounting is defect detection threshold management through reviews based on upstream quality accounting. Upstream quality accounting is used to record and graph the defect count for each defect injection phase of each review. This makes it possible to visualize the trends in defect counts with each review.
- If the defect count per defect injection phase does not increase or decrease with each review, then it can be determined that there is a problem in the quality of that defect injection phase. For this reason, it is possible to quickly respond to quality problems not only in that process, but in processes further upstream as well. If upstream quality accounting is not implemented, then it will be difficult to detect

quality problems in processes further upstream, and this will result in the problems slipping into the testing processes, causing major regression.

- The defect injection phase information for the upstream quality accounting's defects can be used to identify problem processes where the quality built in by the organization is poor. For this reason, it has the effect of promoting the improvements in development technology necessary for resolving work output quality problems in those problem processes.

- Another strength of quality accounting is how it can be used to set exit criteria in software testing with absolute certainty. Although this technique was not established during the first stage, it was used to successfully maintain a low level of post-release defect counts starting in the third stage. Since definite exit criteria in software testing could be set, this made it possible to prevent quality problems that could lead to recurring issues on the customer's side after shipment before they occurred, and so the low post-release defect count was successfully maintained.

- Not only does the promotion of quantification through quality accounting encourage improvements in the quality of developed software, it also makes the organization's overall yearly trends and other such information possible to grasp, which in turn has the effect of leading to long-term improvements in the entire organization. Organization A has been continuously analyzing annual development data for more than 20 years, including the organization's strengths and weaknesses, which have been incorporated into annual improvement plans. These analyses have been tied in with continuous quality improvement activities, as shown in Fig. 7-5.

7.3   Organization B Quality Improvement Example

This section describes an example of an organization suffering from high post-release defect counts (referred to as "Organization B" below), which revised the method of applying quality accounting based on the technique's original aims, thereby succeeding in improving quality. Organization B's business environment resembles that of Organization A in some ways, and so it formulated its improvement measures while using Organization A as a benchmark. This example covers internal corporate improvement activities that were implemented between 2008 and 2012, and in particular, the result of improvements from when they started until 2011, four years later. The author has been serving as the leader of Organization B's improvement activities.

113

7.3.1   Overview of Organization A and Organization B

Both Organization A and Organization B are members of the NEC group, and they develop general-purpose software products for use in IT products in different business regions. The customer segments of both organizations are in roughly the same enterprise area, and the organizations have approximately the same scope in terms of shipment volume, the amount of development carried out, and so on. Both organizations have around 2,000 software engineers, and both use a distributed development system that includes offshore development. Since the two organizations used to be a single organization that was later split, they apply roughly the same software processes. Both Organization A and Organization B achieved CMMI Level 5 near the beginning of the 2000s. The organizations both mainly apply the V model, and are implementing V&V. Development techniques such as designing and testing are also generally the same, and both organizations have adopted the software quality accounting technique [3-9] invented by NEC as their quality management technique.

7.3.2 State of Post-release Defect Count before Improvements

The post-release defect counts (relative values before improvements) of Organization A and Organization B are shown in Fig. 7-6. The post-release defect counts are shown using relative values, with one year of post-release defect counts at Organization A set as 100 in order to show Organization B's relative post-release defect counts. The same year of data for post-release defect counts are shown for both Organization A and Organization B (before improvements) in Fig. 7-6.

When average values are compared, with Organization A's post-release defect counts set to 100, Organization B's post-release defect counts (before improvements) amounted to 236.78, or more than twice the number as occurred at Organization A. Organization B's high post-release defect counts were a problem that actually rose to the level of a business issue, and provided impetus for Organization B's quality improvement activities. After comparative analysis with Organization A, Organization B set the reduction of post-release defect counts to a level equivalent to Organization A after five years as a target.

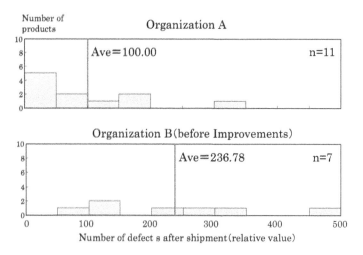

Fig. 7-6 Comparison of Post-release Defect Count between Organization A and Organization B (before Improvements)

("Post-release Defect Count [relative value]" refers to the number of defects occurring at the customer's side in one year, with the average value at Organization A set to 100.)

7.3.3   Result of Improvements

The improvement results achieved in the four years since Organization B started its improvement activities are shown in Fig. 7-7. The conditions are the same as in Fig. 7-6, with relative values given using one year of Organization A's post-release defect counts set as 100. In order to show the history of the improvements, data is provided for Organization B before the improvements, and then three and four years after the start of implementation of improvement measures. Data is used for the same seven products. The data for one and two years after improvements were started is omitted because it is greatly dispersed, which makes it difficult to grasp trends. Since Organization B is a large-scale development organization with 2,000 software engineers, including those working overseas, it took a certain amount of time for improvement measures to permeate to the extent that the effects became evident.

As shown in Fig. 7-7, the average post-release defect count was 236.78 before the improvements, and was reduced to 199.62 after three years, and to 133.78 after four years. At that time, there were no more products at Organization B with a post-release defect count (relative value) of 450 to 500, and whereas there was only one product before the improvements under 100, there were three such products afterwards.

At present, Organization B seems to be well on its way towards achieving the goal of a post-release defect count equivalent to that of Organization A.

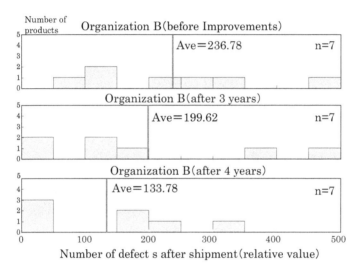

Fig. 7-7 Improvements in Organization B

("Post-release Defect Count [relative value]" refers to the number of defects occurring at the customer's side in one year, with the average value at Organization A set to 100.)

7.3.4   Analysis of Improvement Measures and Implementation Results

In setting Organization A's level as a benchmark, Organization B analyzed the notable differences between Organization B and Organization A, and formulated and implemented improvement measures based on the results of this analysis. The main improvement measures and their results are described below.

Table 7-1 shows the data item definitions used for the formulation of Organization B's improvement plans as well as the analysis of their results. Table 7-2 shows data for before the improvements at Organization A and Organization B, as well as for three and four years after improvement activities began. Other than upstream defect detection rate (No. 9) and success rate of 1+n procedure (No. 10), the data items in Table 7-2 are normalized by scale (KLOC), and are shown relative to the values of the same items for No. 1 through No. 10 at Organization A, with average values at Organization A set as 100. The results of analyses of the validation of differences in population means when there is a correspondence in data for each data item before and after Organization B's improvements with a confidence coefficient of 95% are shown in Table 7-3.

Fig. 7-8 is a scatter plot of the design and coding efforts, review efforts, and test efforts of both Organization A and Organization B with respect to post-release defect count. The top row of Fig. 7-8 shows scatter plots of Organization A and Organization B (before improvements) that were used during formulation of improvement measures, and the bottom row shows scatter plots of Organization B before improvements, three years later, and four years later, that were used to analyze improvement results. Table 7-4 shows information regarding the regression lines shown in Fig. 7-8.

Table 7-1. Data items

No.	Data item	Unit	Definition
1	Total effort	Person-hours/KL	Total person-hours needed to develop Total effort = Design and coding effort (No. 2) + Review effort (No. 3) + Testing effort (No. 4)
2	Design and coding effort	Person-hours/KL	Person-hours needed for design and coding
3	Review effort	Person-hours/KL	Person-hours needed for design or code review
4	Testing effort	Person-hours/KL	Person-hours needed for testing
5	Total defect	Number of defects/KL	Total number of defects detected before shipment Total defect = Defect during review (No. 6) + Defect during testing(No. 7)
6	Defect during review	Number of defects/KL	Of the Total defect (No. 5), the number of defects detected during upstream processes (design, coding and review) before the testing starts. Defects are mainly detected during design or code review in the upstream processes, so this number is called "Defect during review".
7	Defect during testing	Number of defects/KL	Of the Total defect (No. 5), the number of defects detected after testing starts. Defects are mainly detected by testing in the test process, so this number is called "Defect during testing".
8	Testing item	Number of test Items/KL	Number of testing items
9	Upstream defect detection rate	%	Ratio of the Defect during review(No.6) to Total defect (No. 5)
10	Success rate of 1+n procedure	%	"1+n procedure" is a quality improvement measure by detecting same-type defects if a defect is detected in the customer field. 1+n procedure performed where one or more same-type defects are detected is success. Success rate of 1+n procedure = number of "1+n procedure" success cases / number of all "1+n procedure" performed cases

KL = Thousand lines of source code

Table 7-2 Data List

No.	Data item	Organization A					Organization B														
							Before Improvements					After 3 years					After 4 years				
		N	Ave	Min	Max	SD	N	Ave	Min	Max	SD	N	Ave	Min	Max	SD	N	Ave	Min	Max	SD
1	Total effort	11	100.00	37.78	149.51	30.17	7	67.63	50.97	107.27	20.75	7	100.86	62.76	216.42	54.33	7	128.59	82.37	204.48	45.03
2	Design and coding effort	11	100.00	43.38	151.59	30.57	7	99.60	64.28	156.65	99.60	7	150.70	84.03	330.92	94.37	7	118.63	78.33	172.44	37.79
3	Review effort	11	100.00	52.12	152.90	31.22	7	47.00	35.91	61.12	9.76	7	81.48	57.66	119.74	22.92	7	113.62	67.34	177.06	35.52
4	Testing effort	11	100.00	35.81	147.47	33.79	7	48.46	39.53	82.10	15.24	7	67.35	45.46	154.45	39.45	7	139.86	70.64	249.32	62.16
5	Total deffect	11	100.00	73.83	131.25	17.61	7	80.84	64.01	115.01	15.94	7	87.43	78.45	104.73	9.62	7	117.70	82.61	161.52	24.85
6	Defect during review	11	100.00	73.31	131.20	18.81	7	63.07	46.04	101.57	17.95	7	80.25	72.62	96.82	7.97	7	110.53	77.52	145.37	22.45
7	Defect during testing	11	100.00	74.44	131.58	18.31	7	187.77	137.74	284.89	46.48	7	130.68	75.56	181.07	34.30	7	160.91	113.26	258.80	49.74
8	Testing item	11	100.00	56.11	172.78	34.56	7	57.56	18.64	84.14	23.80	7	129.75	35.97	237.66	69.64	7	187.56	115.00	264.22	52.47
9	Upstream defect detection rate	11	100.00	94.56	105.91	2.60	7	77.61	57.60	88.47	9.55	7	92.15	85.72	100.79	5.02	7	94.21	90.15	100.01	3.50
10	Success rate of 1+n procedure	11	100.00	0.00	214.59	66.83	7	46.50	0.00	128.76	54.99	7	83.20	0.00	160.94	52.87	7	123.56	71.53	214.59	44.01

(All figures are relative values, with averages for Organization A set as 100)

Table 7-3 Validation Results of Differences in Population Mean Values between Organization B (before Improvements) and Organization B (after Three and Four Years)

No.	Data item	Before Improvements			After 3 years					After 4 years				
		Average	Dispersion	Standard deviation	Average	Dispersion	Standard deviation	t value	P value (two-sided)	Average	Dispersion	Standard deviation	t value	P value (two-sided)
1	Total effort	67.63	430.71	20.75	100.86	2951.37	54.33	-2.496	0.047	128.58	2027.93	45.03	-3.785	0.009
2	Design and coding effort	99.60	1452.24	38.11	150.70	8905.22	94.37	-2.193	0.071	118.63	1427.72	37.79	-1.408	0.209
3	Review effort	47.00	95.23	9.76	81.48	525.08	22.91	-3.950	0.008	113.62	1261.97	35.52	-5.109	0.002
4	Testing effort	48.46	232.19	15.24	67.35	1556.57	39.45	-2.055	0.086	139.86	3863.95	62.16	-3.611	0.011
5	Total deffect	80.84	253.97	15.94	87.43	92.46	9.62	-0.763	0.474	117.70	617.65	24.85	-6.225	0.001
6	Defect during review	63.07	322.30	17.95	80.25	63.48	7.97	-2.115	0.079	110.53	504.13	22.45	-7.462	0.000
7	Defect during testing	187.77	2160.70	46.48	130.68	1176.68	34.30	3.301	0.016	160.91	2474.06	49.74	1.341	0.229
8	Testing item	57.56	566.56	23.80	129.75	4850.07	69.64	-3.255	0.017	187.56	2753.56	52.47	-7.063	0.000
9	Upstream defect detection rate	77.61	91.23	9.55	92.15	25.19	5.02	-6.092	0.001	94.21	12.22	3.50	-4.608	0.004
10	Success rate of 1+n procedure	46.50	2519.94	50.20	83.20	2794.97	52.87	-1.085	0.319	120.50	1965.69	44.34	-4.101	0.006

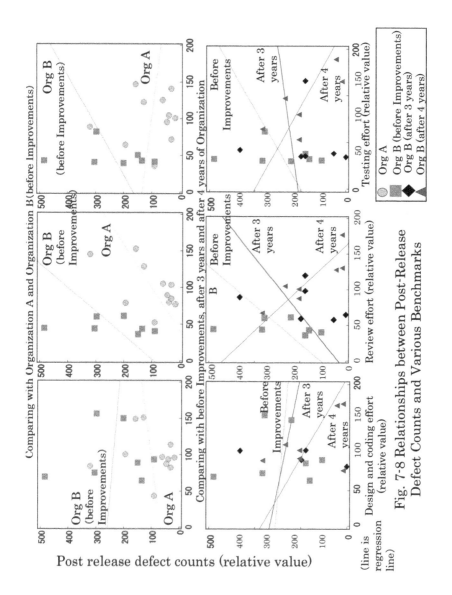

Fig. 7-8 Relationships between Post-Release
Defect Counts and Various Benchmarks

121

Table 7-4 Results of Analysis of Regression Lines in Fig. 7-8 Scatter Plots

No	Item	Design and coding effort and defect after shipment				Review effort and defect after shipment				Testing effort and defect after shipment			
		Org A	Org B			Org A	Org B			Org A	Org B		
			Before Improvements	After 3 years	After 4 years		Before Improvements	After 3 years	After 4 years		Before Improvements	After 3 years	After 4 years
1	Coefficient of correlation	0.109	-0.064	-0.273	-0.493	0.573	0.221	0.262	-0.867	-0.122	0.165	0.079	-0.779
2	Cnstant term of regression	66.693	259.546	279.094	309.644	-70.878	92.193	29.724	449.232	133.716	165.494	175.012	332.993
3	Coefficient of regression	0.333	-0.229	-0.527	-1.482	1.709	3.076	2.085	-2.776	-0.337	1.471	0.365	-1.424
4	t value	0.330	-0.144	-0.636	-1.266	2.098	0.507	0.608	-3.899	-0.370	0.375	0.178	-2.776
5	P value (two-sided)	0.749	0.891	0.553	0.261	0.065	0.633	0.570	0.011	0.720	0.723	0.866	0.039

(1)   Strengthening reviews and tests

Table 7-2 compares Organization A and Organization B (before improvements). The average value for design and coding efforts is 99.60 for Organization B (before improvements), with the same value for Organization A set to 100, or roughly the same (No. 2 in Table 7-2). On the other hand, Organization B's review efforts were at 47.00 before the improvements, its test efforts were at 48.46, and its number of test items was at 57.56, or approximately half of Organization A's 100 (refer to Nos. 3, 4, and 8 in Table 7-2). Although the detected defect count for reviews is low at 63.07, the detected defect count for tests is high at 187.77, or almost twice as high as for Organization A (refer to Nos. 6 and 7 in Table 7-2). These results indicate that although Organization B was focusing sufficient efforts on design and coding before the improvements, defect detection during reviews was insufficient, and this caused there to be a large number of defects remaining at the start of testing, such that one could infer that the number of defects detected was high even with fewer tests.

Next, the graphs in the top row of Fig. 7-8 can be used to analyze the relationship between the post-release defect count and each data item at Organization A and Organization B (before improvements). Much of the data distributed throughout the scatter plot for design and coding efforts in the upper left corner of Fig. 7-8 overlaps between Organization A and Organization B (before improvements). When it comes to review and test efforts, however, it is evident that the data for Organization A and Organization B (before improvements) is distributed with almost no overlap (see the middle and right graphs in the top row of Fig. 7-8). This trend is also clear in the slope of the regression lines. In particular, in the test effort and post-release defect count scatter plot, the slope for Organization A shows a downward trend moving to the right, indicating that the more tests are performed, the lower the post-release defect count tends to be. For Organization B (before improvements), on the other hand, the trend moves in the opposite direction (see the graph in the upper right corner in Fig. 7-8 and Table 7-4).

As described in section 7.2, Organization A invented and applied software quality accounting in the past, and strengthened defect detection based on reviews, thereby reducing the number of post-release defects per year to 1/20th of the previous level. This detection of defects through reviews is a characteristic of software quality accounting techniques, and the upstream defect detection rate representing the effectiveness of this defect detection through reviews exceeded 80% during Organization A's period of making improvements.

Based on the results of its analysis of Organization A and Organization B (before improvements), as well as the experiences of Organization A, Organization B decided to implement improvement measures based on strengthening both reviewing and testing. The data acquired as a result of these measures is shown in Table 7-2 for three and four years after Organization B started making its improvements.

In order to statistically verify the significant differences exhibited in the changes in numerical values before and after Organization B's improvements, Table 7-3 shows the results of validating the difference in population means when there is a correspondence in the data for each data item's average value. After analysis with a confidence coefficient of 95% and a significance level of 5%, the five data items of total effort, review effort, count of defects detected during tests, number of test items, and upstream defect detection rate were shown to have a significant difference between values for Organization B (before improvements) and Organization B (after three years). In addition, a significant difference was found in the average values for Organization B (after four years) relative to Organization B (before improvements) for the eight data items other than design and coding efforts, and count of defects detected during tests. Based on these results, the improvement outcome after three years of improvement activities is seen in half of the data items, and this outcome is even greater after four years. The two data items for which no significant difference was found in the change of the numerical values were design and coding effort and count of defects detected during tests. The reason for this in the case of design and coding effort was that no direct improvement activities were implemented in the areas of design and coding. The count of defects detected during tests is considered below.

After Organization B implemented improvements in both reviewing and testing, data items were analyzed where a significant difference in average values was seen. Increases were seen in both review effort and the number of test items three years after improvements were begun. As a result, the count of defects detected during tests decreased, and the upstream defect detection rate increased in relative terms. This indicates that the increase in the number of defects detected during reviews caused the number of defects remaining at the start of testing to decrease, in such a way that even when the number of test items increased, the number of defects detected during testing still decreased. Four years after the start of improvements, in addition to both review effort and the number of test items, test effort also increased. As a result, the count of defects detected during reviews increased, as did the total detected defect count. Based on this outcome, it can be said that Organization B's activities strengthening both reviews and tests were effective.

Certain issues are also apparent. The count of defects detected during tests for Organization B (after four years) is still high at 160.91, and no statistically significant difference was seen between this value and the value before the improvements. Although this value had fallen to 130.68 for Organization B (after three years), it increased again by the fourth year. This is thought to be due to a large number of defects remaining at the start of testing, in comparison with Organization A (see No. 7 in Table 7-2). Since the total detected defect count of Organization B (after four years) was high at 117.70, this indicates that there is a need to improve the quality of design itself (see No. 5 in Table 7-2). Although these improvement activities did not include design or coding, they are thought to reflect the necessity for improvements in these areas.

Although these measures to strengthen reviewing and testing have shown an effect, values are high for Organization B (after four years) in both review effort (113.62) and test effort (139.86) when compared to Organization A, and this indicates the need for streamlining in addition to an increase in defect detection through greater efforts (see Nos. 3 and 4 in Table 7-2).

The next point to consider is how the total effort of Organization B (after four years) has increased to 128.59 (see No. 1 in Table 7-2). This increase in total effort represents a reduction in productivity defined as the effort applied towards development by unit scale. This reduction in productivity may grow into a major business-level issue in the future. Before Organization B made its improvements, 1) it did not apply an appropriate level of effort to its development, and as a result 2) it suffered from a large number of post-release defects, all of which required effort to handle, and both of these points were seen as problems. It is difficult, however, to determine what the "appropriate level" mentioned in the first point is. This determination must be based on the technology of the organization's development teams, and the post-release defect count. In the case of Organization B, the post-release defect count was seen as an issue, and it was determined based on a comparative analysis with Organization A that both reviewing and testing were insufficient. This should be interpreted to mean that an appropriate level of effort was not being applied based on the technology of the organization's development teams and the required post-release defect count. With respect to the second point, however, Organization B's post-release defect count is decreasing, which means that this problem is heading in the direction of resolution. In general, when the post-release defect count is high, even if the effort applied to each unit of development during the period between the start of development and shipment is increased, when the period after shipment through the maintenance stage is compared, the total effort is thought to decrease, not increase. Based on the measurement results for the organization to which the author belongs, the effort required to correct one post-release defect is at least 100 times as large as the effort required during the design or coding stage. The longer it takes after shipment until the defect becomes evident, the fewer developers there will be available who directly worked on the function in which that defect exists, and so the effort required to correct the defect will increase due to a lack of information regarding the development. Therefore, it is thought that if as in the case of Organization B, the count of defects detected during reviews is increased through improvement activities in order to decrease the post-release defect count, causing the total effort to increase, the total cost will still not go up when maintenance efforts after shipment are also considered. Regardless, the streamlining of reviews and tests is seen as one of the issues for Organization B to contend with in the future, and is an item that should always be kept in mind.

The next area to consider is the trend in data items concerning Organization B's post-release defect count as shown in the scatter plots in the bottom row of Fig. 7-8, before improvement, three years after improvements began, and four years after improvements began. The scatter plot for design and coding efforts in the lower left corner of Fig. 7-8 shows data distributions that are roughly overlapping for Organization B (before improvements), Organization B (after three years), and Organization B (after four years). On the other hand, although there is no major difference between the review effort and test effort distributions for Organization B (before improvements) and Organization B (after three years), it is clear that the trend is changing in Organization B (after four years). An examination of the trends in the regression lines for Organization B (after four years) shows that the review effort and the post-release defect count are sloping downward to the right (see the bottom middle graph in Fig. 7-8 and Table 7-4). This indicates that the more reviews are conducted, the more the post-release defect count decreases. A similar trend is evident in test effort (see the bottom right graph in Fig. 7-8 and Table 7-4). These results also show that Organization B's improvement activities strengthening reviewing and testing were effective.

(2)   Strengthening implementation of the "defect root cause analysis and 1+n procedure" technique

"Defect root cause analysis and 1+n procedure", which is one technique of software quality accounting, was also being implemented at Organization B before the improvements. The effectiveness of the "defect root cause analysis and 1+n procedure" is measured by the yardstick calculated from the following 1+n procedure success rate formula:

1+n procedure success rate (%) = (number of 1+n procedure implementation cases with one or more same-type defect detected / total number of 1+n procedure implementation cases) × 100.

The goal of the "defect root cause analysis and 1+n procedure" technique is the detection of same-type defects. For this reason, "defect root cause analysis and 1+n procedure" implementation cases where a same-type defect was detected are treated as successes in the above success rate formula, and cases where no same-type defect was detected are treated as failures.

When Table 7-2 is referenced, the average value of the Organization B 1+n procedure success rate before improvements is 46.50, or approximately half that of Organization A. Although, just as at Organization A, Organization B has made the implementation of the "defect root cause analysis and 1+n procedure" technique to the defect root cause analysis of post-release defects occurring at the customer's side obligatory, same-type defects were not being detected, and the technique was not having an effect. This can also be observed in Fig. 7-9. Organization A's regression line shows a downward-sloping trend to the right, and the higher the same-type defect success rate, the lower the post-release defect count. For Organization B, on the other hand, both the post-release defect count and the 1+n procedure success rate showed the opposite trend, or upward to the right (see Fig. 7-9 and Table 7-5). Reasons for this lack of effectiveness include the fact that Organization B's defect root cause analysis method was a special "five whys analysis" technique instead of software quality accounting's "defect root cause analysis", as well as the fact that there were cases where the 1+n procedure was not tied to the results of defect root cause analysis.

As part of its improvement activities, Organization B once again made it obligatory to apply the "defect root cause analysis and 1+n procedure" to severe defects detected during that final stage of testing, and to defects detected on the customer's side post-release. In this example, the organization worked on making improvements in all "defect root cause analysis and 1+n procedure" cases meeting these conditions.

After Organization B began its improvements, the average value of the 1+n procedure success rate was 83.20 after three years, and 123.56 after four years, or 2.6 times as high than before the improvements. The difference between the value before improvements and four years after is also statistically different (see Table 7-3). Fig. 7-9

127

shows that although the post-release defect count and 1+n procedure success rate have not changed much by the third year when compared with trends before the improvements, by the fourth year a clear change can be observed in the trends.

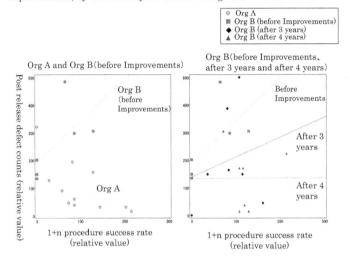

Fig. 7-9 Relationship between Post-release Defects and 1+n Procedure Success Rate

Table 7-5 Results of Analyzing the Regression Lines in Fig. 7-9's Scatter Plots

	Org A	Org B		
		Before Improvements	After 3 years	After 4 years
Coefficient of correlation	-0.651	0.64	0.212	0.003
Cnstant term of regression	190.821	190.829	138.94	132.889
Coefficient of regression	-0.908	1.517	0.729	0.007
t value	-2.576	1.665	0.485	0.006
P value (two-sided)	0.03	0.171	0.648	0.995

The changes in application of the "defect root cause analysis and 1+n procedure" technique at Organization B when compared to before the improvements are described below.

- The quality accounting's defect root cause analysis technique (specifically, the defect root cause analysis sheet shown in Fig. 4-2 of chapter 4 is used) is now applied across the board.

- Education is implemented regarding defect root cause analysis-based quality accounting when the defect root cause analysis technique is applied (develop bases include offshore development in China as well as development scattered around Japan, so education involves visiting all bases).

- A quality assurance department independent from the developing department reviews the validity of defect root cause analysis results produced by the developing department once per year. If analyses are not accurate, then specific guidance is provided.

- At the same time, the quality assurance department reviews the validity of the 1+n procedure formulation details. Since examples have been seen in the past where defect root cause analysis results are not tied to the 1+n procedure, or the scope of the 1+n procedure was reduced for no good reason, the aim is to prevent this type of problem before it happens.

- The quality assurance department reviewed the validity of 1+n procedure implementation results. Where it was determined that same-type defect detection should be continued, reimplementation of the "defect root cause analysis and 1+n procedure" technique was requested.

- Reports in each type of management meeting were made obligatory upon completion of the "defect root cause analysis and 1+n procedure", based on the severity of the defects in the defect root cause analysis. This meant that the results of "defect root cause analysis and 1+n procedure" implementation were to be reviewed from the top, and that information would be shared within the organization.

The reason that Organization B's switch from its own brand of "five whys analysis" to the application of software quality accounting's "defect root cause analysis" was effective is related to the goal-setting of defect root cause analysis, as section 4.6 also considered. Once again, the "five whys analysis" technique can be widely and generally applied in order to analyze root causes. In almost every case, multiple root causes exist for each analyzed defect. For this reason, unless root causes are analyzed with a specific goal in mind, multiple root causes will be analyzed, and it will not be possible to arrive at the desired root cause. Rather than simply repeating the question "why?", it is necessary to keep a specific goal in mind while analyzing root causes to that end. This is why the "defect root cause analysis" part of the "defect root cause analysis and 1+n procedure" technique is a root cause analysis technique that was optimized with the goal of detecting same-type defects. In order to achieve this goal, the following three root cause analysis viewpoints are used in the "defect root cause analysis": defect injection phase of the analyzed defect, cause of injection, and cause of overlook. Furthermore, defect root cause analysis sheets are prepared with a collection of past root causes, and are designed to make analysis easier. This is an extremely goal-oriented technique when compared to the widely applicable "five whys analysis", which does not limit the scope of analysis.

In order to implement the "defect root cause analysis and 1+n procedure" technique, the 1+n procedure success rate must be raised by using important mechanisms that include analysis support through education and a quality assurance department, implementation result review by the top of the organization, and systems for sharing information inside the organization. Organization B has developed mechanisms that act as these foundations at the same time, and this is what resulted in the observed effects.

The various improvements resulting from the implementation of the "defect root cause analysis and 1+n procedure" technique were covered separately in this section for a reason. Improvements in root cause analysis capabilities are said to contribute to improvements in that organization's processes as well [7-1]. This is because the ability to precisely analyze root causes enables that organization to precisely resolve the issues that affect it. Therefore, Organization B's improvement in its 1+n procedure success rate is equivalent to its ability to precisely resolve issues, and improvements in this ability are thought to have acted as the driving force behind Organization B's success in its overall quality improvement measures.

(3)   Implementing evaluation from the customer's perspective by the quality assurance department

Organization B's quality assurance department is an organization that is independent from the development department. Before the improvements were made, the quality assurance department would use the analysis of development data measured during development to grasp the state of development. Evaluation based on verification of the operation of actual development work output was not implemented, however.

Based on these improvement measures, it was decided to have the quality assurance department implement evaluation of the final work output of development from the customer's perspective, in addition to testing by the development department itself. Thanks to this measure, it became possible to actually detect software defects that cannot be grasped simply through quality management based on data during development. Evaluation from the customer's perspective means evaluation following usage scenarios that envision how the customer will use the product.

The effects of evaluation by the quality assurance department from the customer's perspective were major. Of the series of improvement measures, this was the first one to have an effect. The reason for this is because, rather than just indicating problem points in the development data, it demonstrated the existence of problems by detecting defects in the final work output. This measure improved the position of the quality assurance department, and made subsequent improvement measures easier to execute. Also, this implementation of evaluation by the quality assurance department from the customer's perspective accounted for 4% of the detected defects in the count of defects detected during tests (see No. 7 in Table 7-2).

Furthermore, the results of evaluation by the quality assurance department from the customer's perspective were incorporated into the release decision-making standard, which was revised in a number of ways, including the addition of a condition whereby if defects are detected in excess of the threshold, then shipment is halted. Based on this, products with quality problems have actually had their shipments halted, and it has become obligatory to implement improvement measures until a product satisfies release the decision-making standard.

(4)   Measures regarding project management meetings

The methods of holding project management meetings (referred to below as "scheduled meetings"), which are attended by responsible parties at all development departments as well as responsible parties in the quality assurance department, were improved from three angles: face-to-face meetings are now held weekly, the state of development is now discussed based on development data from that week, and the quality assurance department now participates. Before the improvements, although meetings were being held weekly, they were not face-to-face, and the quality assurance department would not participate. Also, development data would be summarized and reported at the end of the process, and the quality assurance department would implement the process phase transition in writing. Ever since the improvements, the quality assurance department now reports and discusses the analysis results based on weekly development data, meetings are face-to-face, and improvements in communication with responsible parties at distributed development bases are thought to be particularly helpful in the early detection of problems during development. When problems that occur during development can be grasped as they occur, all participants in the scheduled meetings can agree on how to proceed regarding solutions, from formulation through implementation. For this reason, a formal written process phase transition is now unnecessary, and more practical follow-ups are now possible. Also, since the system is put together in such a way that thorough weekly follow-ups are possible, this has been an effective means of strengthening follow-ups regarding reviews and tests.

7.3.5   Considerations

The factors that can be seen as important parts of Organization B's success in reducing post-release defect count are described below. All of the efforts mentioned here were achieved through the strict application of quality accounting techniques and the development of mechanisms related to quality accounting.

(1) Promoting a defect detection rate of 80% through reviews

Since Organization B had already been applying quality accounting from before, defect detection through reviews was already firmly established. Due to these improvements, the rate of defect detection through reviews was raised to roughly 80%, and the results shown in Fig. 7-7 were successfully achieved. In previous examples at the organization that invented quality accounting as well, defect detection through reviews was an effective method of improving quality. Furthermore, it is thought that once a detected pre-release defect count of 80% or greater is achieved, this will have a major effect in decreasing the post-release defect count.

(2) Precise exit criteria in software testing

Improvement in the precision of the quality level determination at the time of shipment is an important factor that directly reduces the post-release defect count, but determining whether or not quality can be assured as having reached the prescribed level at the time of shipment is extremely difficult. Organization B was still able to achieve it through the rigorous application of three quality accounting techniques around the end of planned testing (defect trend assessment, defect root cause analysis and 1+n procedure, and defect convergence determination) in combination with evaluation by the quality assurance department from the customer's perspective. If defects in excess of the threshold are detected during implementation of Organization

B's newly established policy of having the quality assurance department evaluate from the customer's perspective, shipment is now treated as not possible under the revised policy, and so the shipment of products with quality problems is always postponed. Furthermore, specific test details are provided based on the results of analysis using quality accounting for the additional testing aimed at resolving the detected quality problems. In particular, with the "defect root cause analysis and 1+n procedure" technique promoting improvements over the course of three years, a same-type defect count was achieved that was 2.6 times as high (see No. 10 in Table 7-2, "1+n procedure success rate, before improvements: 46.50, four years after: 123.56).

(3) Face-to-face management in short cycles based on data

The quality verification based on data used to be implemented at the time of process transition (referred to below as the "process phase transition"). This process phase transition technique is a method that is widely used at software development sites. It is thought, however, that the process phase transition technique often does not have much of an effect in terms of quality improvement. The reason for this is that the details considered during the process phase transition are used to verify the conclusions of problems that occurred during development as well as the results of the end of the process, and are often nothing more than a rubber-stamping of results. Measures must be implemented to grasp problems more quickly after they occur, to more precisely ascertain the true cause of the problems, and to arrive at a conclusion while monitoring the state of the development site.

At the very least, by implementing management based on data on a short weekly cycle, it is possible to become aware of problems soon after they occur. Furthermore, face-to-face meetings improve communication with distributed development bases that never come face-to-face without making a specific effort to do so, and provide the benefit of making it easier to report on-site problems and take action to resolve them early.

In this improvement example, the revision of the operational method for scheduled meetings played an important role in quality improvement.

(4) Upgrading quality assurance mechanisms

In the end, Organization B applied the same quality assurance system as the one used at Organization A (see Fig. 7-10). The addition of weekly data collection, management based on scheduled meetings, evaluation by the quality assurance department from the customer's perspective, and other comprehensive improvements in the software processes throughout the entire development process are thought to have contributed to improvements in quality. Each component of the quality assurance system is indispensable for Organization B. Quality assurance mechanisms differ in their requirements based on the software being developed and the attributes of the customers. Post-release defects must be analyzed in order to upgrade to appropriate quality assurance mechanisms. If many problems seen as severe in software developed by an organization occur on the customer's side, then the quality assurance mechanisms are not sufficient. For instance, this is when in spite of the fact that high reliability is demanded of the software, a large number of defects occur on the customer's side that cause operations to halt. In this case, quality accounting's defect root cause analysis technique is used to analyze the causes of these post-release defects being both injected and overlooked, and mechanisms are revised in order to rework design techniques and otherwise ensure that the causes are prevented before they occur. It is by repeating this procedure that mechanisms can be constructed to ensure quality throughout the entire software product based on the attributes of the organization.

(5) Practical application of a hands-on approach

Quality accounting strongly promotes actually going to the site of development and grasping the actual state of affairs, rather than simply relying on numerical data. The reason for this is that there is a high risk of missing the signs for a variety of different on-site problems if one only relies upon numerical data. This promotion of face-to-face management is also a part of the hands-on approach. When one considers this history of improvements at Organization B, the short-cycle face-to-face management and organized efforts can be seen as leading to improved communication between concerned parties, active exchanges of opinions regarding quality problems, and self-motivated improvement efforts. Although it is difficult to present direct effects of the practical application of this hands-on approach, activities emphasizing facts with deep roots in the development site are thought to contribute to improvements in software quality.

7.4   Offshore Development Organization C Quality Improvement Example

This example describes an example of quality improvements in offshore development as implemented by an NEC subsidiary in China (referred to as "Organization C" below). "Offshore development" refers to the outsourcing of software development to a corporation located overseas.

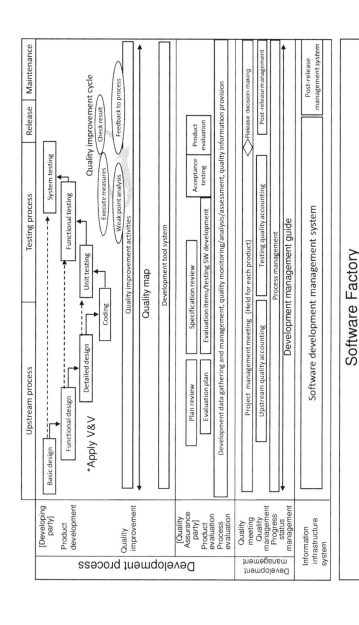

Fig. 7-10 Quality Assurance System of Organization A and B

Many problems occur in offshore development that stem from differences in the software development technologies used at the outsourcing company and at the company located overseas, as well as from differences in languages used to communicate and different cultures. Examples of efforts in these areas have been reported [7-2][7-3][7-4][7-5].

NEC's offshore development in China began in the second half of the 1980s. Before quality improvement activities were begun at the start of the 2000s, Organization C had all the problems often seen in offshore development, including a large number of defects, deadline delays, and poor communication. Organization A, which is Organization C's parent organization, began to sense a crisis due to the lack of any signs of improvement, and based on the determination that unless something was done, Organization A's business might be affected, decided to launch a quality improvement project at Organization C. This quality improvement project, which was active from 2002 to 2004, hit its quality and productivity targets in one year and ten months, successfully achieving quality and productivity in its software development of the same level as development in Japan. The author served as the leader of this quality improvement project.

7.4.1 Organization C Issues

Organization C develops general-purpose software products, and works exclusively on Organization A's development projects. Since the organization works on general-purpose software products, its development involves continuously working on the same product. This characteristic makes it easy to improve technologies with fixed personnel.

Although Organization C had been established approximately ten years before the improvements were begun, the transfer of technologies from Organization A to Organization C did not proceed smoothly, and neither did improvements in quality and productivity, to the extent that unless something changed, it was predicted that both group companies would sustain major losses. The specific problems are described below.

(1) Insufficient management capabilities due to a rapid increase in personnel

In response to Organization A's requests, Organization C rapidly increased its number of engineers starting in 2000, from around 100 to 600. As a result, however, management capabilities were weaker relative to the number of employees. For this reason, the larger numbers of personnel could not be used effectively.

(2) Insufficient development technology of the development team due to advances in work content

Due to the sudden increase in personnel, Organization C now had large numbers of younger engineers with little product development experience, with almost no opportunities to achieve development know-how through on-the-job training (OJT). In addition, the organizational development capabilities required for software development were also lacking. For its part, Organization A lacked offshore development experience, and did not have a method for smoothly transferring technologies overseas.

(3) Lack of communication due to poor Japanese language abilities

Since products are being developed for Japan, engineers are required to have Japanese language abilities, but not many engineers spoke Japanese at an advanced enough level to discuss specifications. This would lead to problems such as engineers not understanding explanations of specifications very well, engineers not being fully informed of changes in the development schedule, late responses, and so on.

7.4.2　Improvement Measures

The aforementioned issues are not limited to just Organization A or just Organization C, but were seen as issues to be tackled by both sides. Also, early improvements were seen as a way to derive larger benefits later. Therefore, the leadership of both Organization A and Organization C decided to cooperate in the launching of activities to improve quality and productivity in Organization C's software development, and began working to improve offshore development. The main improvement measures are described below.

(1) Definition of improvement framework through the step-up model

Two methods for proceeding with improvements are conceivable: the method of promoting a better awareness of improvement in the organization to be improved, so that it works to improve and establish better technologies and mechanisms on its own, and the method of introducing and firmly establishing the use of preexisting technologies and mechanisms at the organization to be improved. In the case of Organization C, the latter method was selected because it was necessary for business reasons to improve Organization C's quality and productivity in a short period of time.

If the former method of having Organization C conceive of its own methods of improving technologies and mechanisms had been selected, a long period of time would have been required to implement these improvements. Organization A's technologies and mechanisms, on the other hand, with their quality accounting core, were already known to be effective, and so it was decided that they could be introduced in order to more easily achieve improvements in a short period of time.

In order to define the overall improvement framework, a "step-up model" was invented in order to steadily transfer technologies and mechanisms in stages, while at the same time improving both quality and productivity (see Fig. 7-11). The step-up model takes technologies and mechanisms that have already been established in Japan and, in a short period of time, introduces and firmly establishes them in an organization engaged in offshore development. By following this model, it is possible to dependably transfer technology in a minimum of 1.5 years, so that Organization C can improve quality and productivity without fail. This step-up model is comprised of the following three stages, and specific numerical targets are set for the ending criteria of each step, including quality, productivity, and Japanese language abilities.

[1] Step 1: "Joint Development"

The goal of this step is the transfer of basic technologies and product knowledge that can be learned through on-the-job training. Joint development teams are formed with members from both Organization A and Organization C, and development is carried out together to the extent possible. Once basic technologies are learned, the large discrepancies in quality and productivity disappear, and quality and productivity can be ensured to be within a certain range. Through software quality accounting, basic technologies also include early quality assurance through reviews, which has been successfully and firmly established at Organization A in an organized fashion.

[2] Step 2: "Semiautonomous Development"

The goal of this step is the transfer of management technologies such as software quality accounting, maintenance technologies, and product development knowledge at a level whereby autonomous development management is possible. Based on the requirement specifications created by Organization A, not only did Organization C implement everything from function design to function testing, it also learned about how to proceed with development through autonomous management. Organization C also mastered development methods based on systemization, such as the implementation of quality improvement measures based on quality analysis results achieved with quality accounting, as well as the implementation of precautionary measures. This made it possible to reliably assure a certain prescribed level of quality and productivity as an organization.

[3] Step 3: "Autonomous Development"

During this step, Organization C autonomously repeats improvements in the development, management, and maintenance technologies as well as product development knowledge mastered up until step 2, so that both quality and productivity would reach the same level as at Organization A. Once step 3 is passed, Organization C becomes an autonomous development organization with the same development capabilities as software organizations inside Japan.

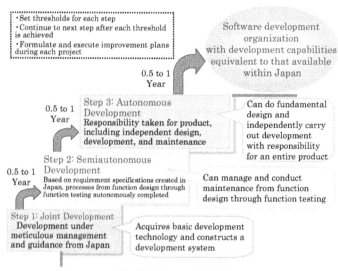

Fig. 7-11 Step-up Model

(2) Detecting and strengthening development weak points through assessment

Assessment sheets were prepared for use in detecting strengths and weaknesses in development, as a tool for supplementing the step-up model that effectively improved the weak points in development. These assessment sheets are comprised of 15 basic items, in the four categories of development work, development management, skill improvement, and facilities/systems (see Fig. 7-12). Each category is evaluated according to the assessment sheet, evaluation points are calculated, and strengths and weaknesses are automatically revealed. Assessment sheets are prepared for three stages in each step of the step-up model, so that evaluation can be performed by Organization A (the organization issuing the work orders) and Organization C (the

139

organization receiving the work orders). This allows weak points to be detected and improvements to be made from both Organization A and Organization C sides.

(3) Promoting standardization

Standardization is implemented by both Organization C and Organization A, and the results are posted to an information-sharing Web site. Organization C upgraded standards throughout the development life cycle, including design specifications, coding rules by language, test specifications, review technologies, test technologies, and others. Organization A upgraded the methods for writing offshore development specifications, progress management methods, and others.

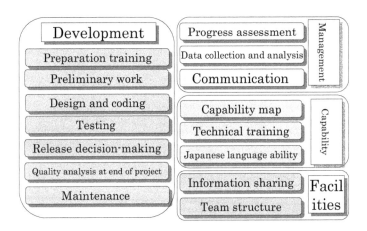

Fig. 7-12 Basic Assessment Model Items

(4) Upgrading infrastructure

The infrastructure that supports offshore development must be upgraded so that it proceeds smoothly. Improvements were supported by upgrading Internet-based remote meeting equipment, information sharing Web and FTP servers, development management tools, and others.

(5) Strengthening Japanese language abilities

Based on a policy of strengthening the Japanese language abilities of engineers throughout Organization C, an effort was made to improve Japanese skills. A Japanese course curriculum was developed with attendance checks, planned long-term business trips to Japan and on-the-job training were implemented, a workplace environment where Japanese is used was developed, and other measures were carried out.

140

(6) Holding regular top management reviews

While proceeding with improvement activities based on a promotional program, the top leadership of Organization A would visit Organization C once every six months, holding a top management review where they would meet face-to-face with Organization C's top leadership and engineers in order to follow up on the state of improvements. These meetings had a major effect, inspiring engineers from both organizations and enabling the improvement cycle to proceed smoothly.

7.4.3   Improvements Results

By one year and ten months after the aforementioned efforts were begun, Organization C's quality and productivity had both improved greatly. The details are described below (see Fig. 7-13).

(1) Quality

The number of defects in Organization C's development work detected at Organization A after delivery was reduced by 85% in comparison with the numbers detected before the improvements, and quality was improved to six times the level at delivery. In addition, the number of cases where the post-release defect count would vary widely based on development conditions also decreased, indicating that Organization C had achieved the capability to develop in a stable manner. All projects exhibited capabilities at or above step 2, and the organization can be responsible for work starting with function design.

(2) Productivity

The amount of development completed per unit time was improved by a factor of three over the amount before the improvements. As standardization proceeded, quality was also improved, efficient development became possible, and regression work was dramatically reduced.

(3) Japanese language abilities

Japanese language certification rates at each level were improved greatly, to 3.4 times the rates before the improvements. Interpretation services became unnecessary during everyday development, and the developers can now create specifications in Japanese. There is a sense in the flow of development that communication is now proceeding smoothly.

(4) Development cost reductions

The cost of development has been greatly reduced in comparison with the cost before the improvements, and the effective utilization rate is improved by 14% over the rate before

141

the improvements. The "effective utilization rate" is calculated by setting the cost of development in Japan to 100%, and subtracting the cost of offshore development (including both the cost of developing offshore and the cost of management from Japan). The monetary amount when the effective utilization rate is converted to money is the amount of the development costs saved by using offshore development. These saved development costs are in excess of 400 million yen per year when compared to the costs that would have been incurred had these improvement activities not been implemented.

7.4.4   Considerations

Organization C's quality improvement example shows that quality improvement is possible for offshore development as well. Also, the fact that the post-delivery defect count is reduced as productivity is simultaneously improved (line/person-hour [H]) is important. Organization C strengthened its reviews from step 1. When reviews are first strengthened, developers on-site often resist because they feel that the reviews will go around the development process. From an engineer's point of view, it is as if they are being prevented from doing the actual coding work because they are stuck doing nothing but reviews instead when they think it is ready for coding. In addition, they feel as if there is a contradiction in the sense that although review times are being increased over what they used to be, deadlines are not being changed, and the engineers are being demanded to improve productivity target values at the same time (in other words, the effort applied to development per unit time is being reduced). There was also a backlash at Organization C during the initial stages of quality improvement activities. In response, a project was selected where the development team had technological capabilities such that it seemed reviewing would be effective, and concentrated support was provided in order to create an early successful example.

Once there was a successful example, effectiveness began to increase through a sort of process of competition. The development teams were convinced, and began actively participating in improvement activities. The increase in reviews does not directly lead to an increase in overall development efforts. In fact, by reliably implementing reviews, regression effort is reduced, and so is overall effort, as Organization C experienced for itself. NEC teaches that one should "pursue quality, and productivity will follow". In fact, it is the application of early quality assurance through strengthened reviewing that enabled the achievement of productivity improvements. The fact that development costs were actually reduced by the improvements in the effective utilization rate is also important.

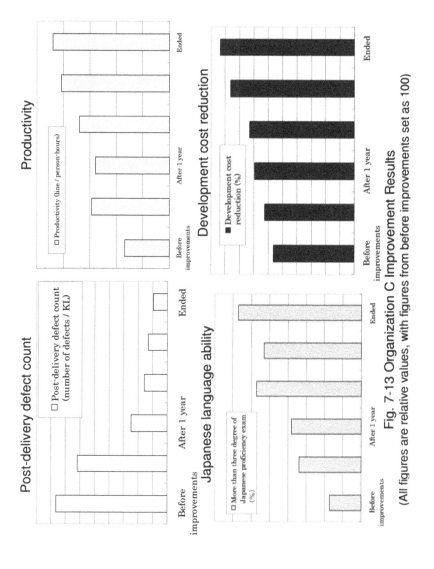

Fig. 7-13 Organization C Improvement Results
(All figures are relative values, with figures from before improvements set as 100)

143

Ever since Organization C completed these quality improvement activities, it has been continuing with additional improvement activities of its own, achieving CMMI Level 5 six months later. More than anything else, this is proof that the step-up model successfully turned Organization C into a software development organization that can develop autonomously.

7.5   Conclusion

This chapter described the three quality improvement examples of Organization A, Organization B, and Organization C. All three examples involved improvement activities that revolved around an axis of software quality accounting. It is particularly important to execute reviews in order to implement early quality assurance, while at the same time supporting the effectiveness of reviews by constructing organized mechanisms to assure quality. Furthermore, in the case of Organization C, it was shown that the strengthening of reviews led to improvements in productivity due to the resulting quality assurance. One of the major causes behind greater effort being required than planned for a software development project is the need for regression work. One typical example of regression work is when a part of the specifications is overlooked, or a design mistake occurs in an upstream process, and the resulting defects are detected in the final test stage, making it necessary to redo design, coding, and testing work. Early quality assurance based on strengthened reviewing effectively reduces this type of regression work. This is why although the strengthened reviewing in the upstream processes appears at first glance to increase the amount of effort required, the overall effort up until shipment actually decreases. This is what enabled the productivity improvements and cost reductions (effective utilization rate improvements) at Organization C.

It is important to focus on just how crucial the construction of organized mechanisms was in all three of these examples. It is difficult to improve the quality level of software development by simply taking one improvement measure, such as strengthening reviews. The entire software development mechanism must also be upgraded at the same time in order to effectively implement improvement measures and successfully achieve quality improvement. Furthermore, it is also important to pay attention to the positive influence the construction of organized mechanisms can have on human factors as well. Changes in the actions taken by engineers were seen during Organization B's period of improvement. Developing organized mechanisms and promoting face-to-face management improved communication between concerned parties and led to an active exchange of opinions regarding quality problems. Although improvements in human factors do not play a direct role, they are still thought to contribute to the creation of a virtuous cycle of quality improvement.

Chapter 8. Engineering Values of Software Quality Accounting

8.1 Introduction

This chapter discusses the engineering values of software quality accounting. Software quality accounting is a quality management technique that revolves around an axis of threshold management based on the defect detection count. The number one value of quality accounting is adopting this easy-to-understand defect detection threshold management method, which makes it easy to introduce quality accounting. Of course, quality accounting has more values than just this type of surface-level value.

The principles of quality accounting were listed in Fig. 3-4 in chapter 3, and are revisited again below. This chapter describes how these principles are realized in quality accounting techniques, and discusses the associated engineering values.

Principle of Quality Accounting
- Do not inject defects. Rapidly detect any injected defects.

Principle of Upstream Quality Accounting
- Detect any injected defects before the next process.
  - Removal rate of 80% in defect injection phase
  - Detect remaining 20% in next process

Principle of Testing Quality Accounting
- Ship after all injected defects have been detected.

Target
- Upstream defect detection rate of 80%.

Fig. 8-1 Principles of Quality Accounting (Revisited) (Identical to Fig. 3-4)

8.2 Early Quality Assurance through Reviews

One of the core ideas of software quality accounting is the promotion of defect detection through reviewing in order to assure quality early in the software life cycle. In the same way that it is more economical to pay off a debt early, before the interest balloons, detecting a defect injected in design or coding early through reviews, before that defect gives birth to multiple additional defects, reduces the amount of regression work required. Quality accounting realized this by inventing upstream quality accounting.

One of the major characteristics of upstream quality accounting is that two items of information are made clear for each defect, and that management is conducted from the angles of both of these items; namely, the defect injection phase and the defect detection phase. Management from the angle of the defect injection phase is the same idea as "headstream" management in the area of quality management. By analyzing the process where the defect in question was injected, the process causing the defect is made clear. A design process that injects a large number of defects is a problematic process for that software, and so it is necessary to once again review the work output of that design process. The fact that this can be detected at an early stage during the upstream process is one of quality accounting's major strengths. Furthermore, as described in the upstream quality accounting principle, the idea of detecting injected defects before the next process means that the influence of injected defects is stopped before the next process, and quality is assured early. This is not just an idea, however. Defect counts are represented as numerical values, and management from both defect injection phase and defect detection phase angles actually makes analysis possible, which is where the value lies.

In a project that is not managed from the perspective of "headstream" management, the further upstream in the design process a cause is located, the more likely it will be that it will be difficult to become aware of that problem before the second half of testing. Unfortunately, at actual sites of development, developers will often not become aware of a problem until the final process, which is system testing. As a result, since design problems are fixed after they are detected during system testing, a large amount of regression work is required. This is because design and coding must be reimplemented, as well as any testing of the parts surrounding the affected area. Many of the cases where a project that had been proceeding smoothly up to that point suddenly suffers from numerous and continuous defects detected in system testing are caused by defects injected during an upstream design phase not being discovered, and development continuing on regardless. Software quality accounting prevents projects from failing due to these kinds of design problems, and achieves quality assurance from an early stage of software development.

With upstream quality accounting, review effort (person-hour [H]/KLOC) and the count of defects detected during reviews (number of items/KLOC) are two matrices that are used to analyze the state of quality assurance. The technologies for determining quality are defect analysis for each injection phase, and quality decision tables. Upstream quality accounting sheets and charts are provided in order to visualize the state of quality assurance.

The 80% upstream defect detection rate is also an important target value for quality accounting. As was shown in the examples of Organization A and Organization B in chapter 7, in the case of both organizations, when the upstream defect detection rate exceeded 80%, the post-release defect count was greatly reduced. Based on these experiences, the upstream defect detection rate of 80% as promoted by quality accounting is thought to be a meaningful threshold for the reduction of post-release defect count.

Although it has been suggested for a long time that quality assurance through reviewing is an important part of software development, there have not been many solid proposals for concrete review management methods that can be applied at the site of software development. Software quality accounting, however, provides a technique and threshold for precisely managing defect detection with reviews. Software quality accounting is a technique for achieving early quality assurance through reviewing, and the 80% upstream defect detection rate target for achieving this can be said to be one concrete threshold that is provided in order to reduce post-release defect count.

8.3 Precise Exit Criteria in Software Testing

The testing quality accounting principle, which is one of the quality accounting principles, states that it is necessary to "ship after all injected defects have been detected". This is an idea that has existed since the invention of quality accounting. Quality accounting is an expansion of the idea that "defects should be thought of as debts that must be repaid before shipment". The provision of an exit criterion in software testing technique to determine whether or not all debts have been repaid is one of the major characteristics of quality accounting.

With quality accounting, in order to apply exit criteria in software testing after all planned tests have been implemented, the three techniques of "defect trend assessment", "defect root cause analysis and 1+n procedure", and "defect convergence determination" are used to analyze the test results. Each one of these three techniques has its own goal. "Defect trend assessment" checks for any major overlooked issues in test viewpoint by analyzing all detected defects from a variety of different viewpoints using stratified analysis. "Defect root cause analysis and 1+n procedure" is applied to important defects detected during the final stage of testing, in order to clarify the reason why they still exist at that point, and to execute countermeasures to deal with the causes. By focusing on each separate defect, the "defect root cause analysis and 1+n procedure" technique prevents important items from being overlooked in tests from specific narrow perspectives. Finally, "defect convergence determination" verifies that defects are actually in a converging trend. When analysis results for all three of these techniques indicate that there is no problem, it is determined that "all debts have been repaid", and testing is complete. "Debt" in this case refers to remaining issues, or in other words, the defects that still exist due to remaining issues.

Meticulousness and accuracy are required in software development. A single oversight can cause a fatal problem. If a fatal problem occurs on the customer's side, then all the quality assurance work up to that point will be for nothing. The three techniques provided by quality accounting are combined in the exit criteria in software testing used to prevent these types of problems in advance. The determination of exit criteria in software testing is a difficult problem for a software development organization. As shown in the example of Organization B (see section 7.3 in chapter 7), the thorough application of quality accounting makes it possible to implement highly precise exit criteria in software testing. The most important characteristic of quality accounting is how testing is judged as finished only after it is determined from three different perspectives that there are no problems remaining. Software is complicated, and has attributes that are both invisible and greatly influenced by human components. It is difficult to determine when testing is complete for software with these types of attributes, if only one-sided results are used to make that determination. This is why it is almost impossible to find a technique that provides an exit criterion in software testing method that is both comprehensive and concrete. Quality accounting's value is in the fact that it provides just such an exit criterion in software testing method.

8.4 Improvement in Issue Resolution Capabilities through Defect Root Cause Analysis

Chapter 4 described the characteristics of the "defect root cause analysis and 1+n procedure" technique. The reason for describing one of the techniques of quality accounting in detail is that the capabilities offered by defect root cause analysis, in particular, greatly influence process improvement.

Engineers who can precisely analyze defect root causes can be said to possess the ability to think in such a way as to consolidate causal relationships of cause and effect based on facts. This ability to analyze the causal relationship between causes and results also leads to the ability to resolve issues during process improvement by precisely analyzing problem points and their causes, and by implementing countermeasures against these causes. When this ability to analyze causal relationships is weak, root cause analysis is often simply based on assumption and speculation. In the example of Organization B as well (see section 7.3 in chapter 7), improvement activities based on misconceptions stemming from speculation were seen before the improvements. For instance, actual cases were occasionally seen where an engineer not in the habit of thinking based on data would implement misplaced improvement activities attacking causes based on his own speculation instead of using an available Pareto chart that showed causes in order of frequency, and would fail to produce results for this reason. It can be inferred, however, that after Organization B started its quality improvement activities, as the 1+n procedure success rate improved, the habit of considering causal relationships while examining data and facts spread, and issue resolution capabilities grew stronger as a result.

Defect root cause analysis based on quality accounting provides analysis methods from the two different perspectives of defect injection cause and overlook cause in order to organize the structure of root causes with the goal of detecting same-type defects. Furthermore, the specific root cause is focused on in the analysis because shared root causes are not effective in the detection of same-type defects. A specific root cause is the direct cause behind a certain defect being injected and overlooked, such as design mistakes based on faulty technological information. A shared root cause is an indirect cause of a certain defect being injected and overlooked, such as a lack of education. Since shared root causes are indirect, even if a measure is implemented against them, there is no guarantee that same-type defects can be detected. The idea of organizing root causes in a structure based on an awareness of the goals of defect root cause analysis can also be applied to aspects of process improvement. Defect root cause analysis is one of the techniques frequently used at the sites of software development. Since, however, the techniques most frequently applied at sites of software development are those general-purpose techniques that can be used in any situation, they cannot efficiently analyze root causes in spite of the amount of time that is spent on them. Although there are many proposals for methods of applying the general-purpose Toyota "five whys" technique to software, almost all of these are just methods of deriving "why" questions, and none of them appear to present an idea regarding how to organize the structure of root causes. Software quality accounting, on the other hand, is very valuable because it does present an idea for how to organize the structure of root causes, and provides a defect root cause analysis technique that narrows the focus down to the detection of same-type defects. Furthermore, defect root cause analysis capabilities cultivated through the application of the "defect root cause analysis and 1+n procedure" technique also contribute to the improvement of process improvement and other general issue resolution capabilities.

8.5 Value as Driver of Quality Improvements

Not only does software quality accounting offer direct effects as a quality management technique, it also has value as a driver of quality improvements. In other words, it plays a guiding role in the promotion of technologies and mechanisms that can identify and resolve weak points in software processes.

The application of quality accounting makes it possible to analyze the state of development by acquiring a variety of different types of data from projects under development, starting with the number of injected defects and the number of detected defects. As a result, it is possible to obtain the strengths and weaknesses of one's own applied technologies and mechanisms. By introducing technologies and mechanisms that can strengthen these weaknesses, it is possible to construct overall quality assurance mechanisms that are centered on quality accounting. This is the value of quality accounting as a driver of quality improvements. Precisely grasping the weaknesses of one's organization as it changes along with the changing business environment and continuously making improvements is the foundation of stable and long-term high-quality software development.

For instance, if a design process has a large number of injected defects, this is an indication that the design technology applied in that process has weak points. Furthermore, by analyzing the details for the specific injected defects, it is possible to identify the weak parts of design technologies, which can then be improved by repeating this process.

Also, by analyzing post-release defect counts, it is possible to identify weak points in software processes in much the same way. In this case, by introducing technologies and mechanisms to resolve these issues, quality accounting is applied and quality assurance mechanisms are developed so that the effectiveness of these measures can be measured during development. This makes it possible to measure the effects of improvements without having to wait until post-release.

As chapter 7 described, Organization A was able to reduce its post-release defect count to 1/20th its previous level more than 20 years ago, and has been maintaining this level ever since. When one considers just how many major changes have occurred in the software industry during this period, including the paradigm shift from mainframes to open systems, the emergence of open source software, and the rise of offshore development, the value of quality accounting as a driver of quality improvements can be seen as tremendously powerful in that it was able to successfully maintain a low post-release defect count throughout this entire time. For instance, during the paradigm shift from mainframes to open systems, environments that could immediately execute a coded program became available at low cost. This convenience became a double-edged sword, however, as there were more and more cases where implementation design or unit testing were carelessly omitted, with the result that problems were occurring frequently during the final test stage, and post-release defects were increasing. The strict application of quality accounting and the overall quality assurance mechanisms based on the technique made it possible to catch the symptoms of these defects and resolve them before they became major problems.

This shows how software quality accounting has value as a driver of quality improvements. By using the quality accounting technique as a driver of quality improvements, it is possible to upgrade the organization's overall software quality assurance mechanism. Although the direct effects of applying quality accounting are also important, its value as a driver of quality improvements provides major benefits from a long-term perspective.

8.6 Emphasizing a Hands-on Approach

The meticulous reviewing of defect forecast values during software development is indispensable for improving the precision of quality accounting application. A variety of different changes occur during software development that could not be foreseen during planning. In addition to changes to the specifications, a number of different problems can occur, such as the inability to secure engineers as planned, the inability to reuse programs as planned, the scale of development growing beyond what was planned, and so on. These problems cannot be forecast reliably in advance, even if risk management is implemented. The key to successful quality accounting is reflecting these changes and revising defect forecast values according to the actual conditions.

In order to revise these detailed defect forecast values, it is absolutely necessary to understand the site on software development. Simply following changes in numerical values is not enough if one is to reflect changes in the actual situation to defect forecast values. There are always reasons for the changes in numerical values, and for gaps between the plan and the actual situation. Defect forecast values can only be revised based on reality if an understanding is achieved of the real reasons for these discrepancies.

Quality accounting emphasizes a hands-on approach because such an approach directly influences the application precision of quality accounting itself. In other words, without the emphasis on a hands-on approach, the application of quality accounting will become a formality, and this will prevent it from succeeding. Attempting to revise defect forecast values according to reality while applying quality accounting should lead inevitably to a hands-on approach.

It goes without saying that this emphasis on a hands-on approach will greatly influence the realization of high-quality software development. In other words, it will directly lead to judgments based on actual conditions, such as whether or not effectiveness is being increased not simply in form but rather in substance, and why effectiveness is being increased.

Software quality accounting demands a hands-on approach. A hands-on approach is mandatory if the application of quality accounting is to succeed.

8.7 Conclusion

This chapter discussed the engineering values of the software quality accounting technique.

Software quality accounting provides five values, all of which are hard to find in other techniques: early quality assurance through reviews, precise exit criteria in software testing, improved issue resolution capabilities through defect root cause analysis, value as a driver of quality improvements, and emphasis on a hands-on approach. What is important is that software quality accounting is constructed at the actual site of development, and that multiple organizations are producing actual results with the technique.

Many of the individual techniques that make up software quality accounting are used frequently at the site of software development. Defect root cause analysis, defect trend assessment, and defect convergence determination are good examples of this. The values of software quality accounting have been put together in such a way that the results of applying each individual technique can be used on-site through detailed feedback, and values are created by combining each technique. All of the values described above are created as results of this process.

The content described in this chapter has been demonstrated by a large-scale development organization with several thousand employees, over more than 20 years. This can be seen as the most important value of all.

Chapter 9. Success Factors of High-Quality Software Development

9.1 Introduction

This chapter discusses the factors behind successful high-quality software development, based on the arguments presented up to chapter 8.

High-quality software development must be considered based on the two aspects of management, at the organization and project levels. To achieve high-quality software development once, it is sufficient to implement management at the project level, but to ensure that all software development projects implemented by the organization have a high probability of being high-quality, efforts at the organizational level are mandatory.

As a precondition for an organization to be able to apply the measures proposed in this chapter, it must be comprised of engineers with a certain level of development skills and discipline necessary for software development. This is not just limited to software development; it goes without saying that any engineers involved in any form of development are required to have a certain level of development skills and discipline. The reason this is explicitly mentioned here is that the current software industry has become a labor-intensive industry, leading to a trend whereby there is always the possibility that the developers with lower rates will be given preference during selection by clients.

9.2 Success Factors and Overall Picture of High-Quality Software Development

There are always multiple software development projects underway at a software development organization. Each project satisfies prescribed QCD targets while concentrating on developing its own work output. The management that ensures this happens is project level management. The organization, on the other hand, concentrates on ensuring that high-quality software development occurs at a high rate of probability in all the projects implemented at that organization. The management that ensures this happens is organization level management.

Figure 9-1 shows the overall picture of success factors behind high-quality software development. There are eight success factors behind high-quality software development.

Organization level management is comprised of three success factors: 1) setting quality improvement targets based on external benchmarks, 2) process improvement based on follow-up on quality improvement targets, and 3) provision of systems integrating software development methodologies, tools, and development environments. Project level management is comprised of five success factors affecting design, coding, and testing in software development processes: 1) early quality assurance through reviews, 2) implementation of testing with precise exit criteria in software testing, 3) short cycle management based on data, 4) quality confirmation from both process and product angles using independent quality assurance departments, and 5) release decision-making by multiple people.

The success factors behind project level management are executed in each project. The success factors behind organization level management are executed at the organization level. For the projects implemented by an organization to have a high probability of achieving high-quality software development, even if there's a difference in how well they are executed, all eight of these success factors are required.

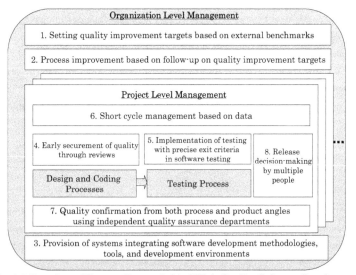

Fig. 9-1 Overview of Success Factors behind High-Quality Software Development

9.3 Success Factors of Management at the Organization Level

Organization level management has as its goal the improvement of the success rate of projects executed by that organization (see section 2.4.3 in chapter 2). Each one of the items described in this section must be executed with this goal of organization level management in mind.

[1] Setting quality improvement targets based on external benchmarks

An organization's quality improvement target setting is important for deciding the direction for quality improvement activities. Quality improvement activities should be planned with the goal of conforming to customer needs, which are an external standard. Therefore, quality improvement targets should adopt external benchmarks that reflect customer opinions, and so ideally both sales and numbers of complaints should be used as targets in a set. This is because if the provided products and services are supported by customers, then sales should increase and complaints should decrease or maintain a low level. Also, due to the nature of the benchmarks, targets should be set at least over a period of several years.

The post-release defect count for objects that are subject to quality aspect evaluation is one typical candidate for use as a quality improvement target. What is important is that an external benchmark with results that the developing organization cannot control is set as the target. The adoption of a benchmark that does not reflect the opinion of the customer as a quality improvement target is not appropriate. Although benchmarks that the developing organization can control during development, such as review effort or the number of test items, are suited towards use as process improvement targets for quality improvement, they are not suited towards use as actual quality improvement targets.

Also, quality improvement targets should be set with the agreement of the organization's top executives. After this, the first step towards achieving high-quality software development is to have the organization's top executives continuously express to the constituent members of the organization a strong intention to meet the quality improvement targets.

[2] Process improvement based on follow-up on quality improvement targets

By analyzing the gap between quality improvement targets and actual values, it is possible to implement the construction or revision of a process if functional omissions or insufficient items are discovered. CMMI, the de facto standard of software process improvement, is worth referencing when this happens. CMMI defines 22 process areas, and presents detailed characteristics, goals, and practices for each one. While referencing CMMI, it is possible to construct each necessary process by implementing the process area mechanisms that are thought to be lacking or insufficient.

Root cause analysis is applied in order to analyze the root causes of problem points. When the root cause is analyzed as in software quality accounting's "defect root cause analysis and 1+n procedure", it is necessary to keep organization of the root cause structure in mind during analysis. The goal of this analysis is linking to process improvement, and so the causes of omitted or insufficient processes are analyzed. The precision of root cause analysis is directly connected to the effects of process improvement.

Rather than just revising a process, it is important to verify that the constructed process is effective. Determine at this point whether or not the quality improvement target set in [1] has been reached. Monitor whether or not problems that must be resolved are truly resolved over the course of several years, and if the resolution is insufficient, revise the process again. Repetition of these steps will lead to process construction that is effective, and not simply a formality.

When it comes to process improvements, it is important to take the Japanese "kaizen" approach. "Kaizen" is not a simple one-time process revision, but rather a constant effort to revise everyday processes while thinking of methods that might be better than the current methods. All of an organization's members participate in "kaizen", from top to bottom. This approach is the foundation of high-quality software development.

[3] Provision of systems integrating software development methodologies, tools, and development environments

The Software Factory described in chapter 6 is envisioned as the "systems integrating software development methodologies, tools, and development environments". Processes revised based on the results of "[2] process improvement based on follow-up on quality improvement targets" are all reflected in the integrated systems that are provided to the developers in this success factor.

Software development methodologies, tools, and development environments greatly influence quality improvement in software development. It is difficult for people to perfectly execute the meticulousness and accuracy required for software development, where not even a single character can be mistaken. Even if people pay the utmost attention to their work, it is still difficult to completely guarantee meticulousness and accuracy in their work. That is why integrated system should be used to guarantee the work, rather than expecting humans to do so. Instead, this allows engineers to use their capabilities to create the concepts behind software, and to demonstrate the correctness of these concepts. This is where the aim of the system lies.

Integrated systems can also be provided for single-project activities. Continuously improving and providing systems is difficult without efforts at the organization level, however. The author has experienced situations where even after an advanced system is constructed for a single project, since it could not be continuously improved, it would fall far behind systems constructed later at the organization level. Unless measures suited for efforts at the organization level are taken on by the organization, it will not be possible to produce the prescribed results.

9.4　Success Factors of Management at the Project Level

The goal of project level management is achieving the QCD demanded of that project. The items described in this section are executed with this goal of project level management in mind.

[1] Early quality assurance through reviews

Defect detection is implemented with an emphasis on quality assurance in design and coding processes. All three of the examples discussed in chapter 7 used early defect detection through reviews to reduce the post-release defect count. In the example of Organization C, by strengthening reviews, regression work was reduced, and both an improvement in productivity (line/person-hour [H]) and a reduction in development costs were achieved. In the examples of Organization A and Organization B, once the upstream defect detection rate reached 80%, the post-release defect count fell further. Review-based defect detection is effective for early quality assurance, as well as for reducing the post-release defect count. In particular, the post-release defect count is thought to decrease greatly once this rate exceeds 80%. This approach of emphasizing review is one of the characteristics of Japanese corporations [5-5].

For an organization that is not used to reviewing, the decision to strengthen reviews is extremely difficult. This is because strengthening reviews means increasing efforts in the design and coding processes, and invokes the risk of directly reducing productivity (line/person-hour [H]) and delaying delivery. One example that can motivate the decision to strengthen reviewing is that of Organization C and its offshore development (see section 7.4 in chapter 7). Organization C reduced regression work by strengthening review, and successfully reduced development costs as a result. Only the top executives of an organization can make the decision to strengthen reviewing.

[2] Implementation of testing with precise exit criteria in software testing

Testing does not mean simply implementing planned tests and then finishing. It means always verifying the sufficiency of implemented tests, and using exit criteria in software testing. With exit criteria in software testing, the verification of sufficiency from a diverse range of perspectives is mandatory. With a one-sided perspective, there will always be the risk of flawed judgment. In software quality accounting, the exit criteria in software testing are based on three types of analysis of defects detected in testing: oversights in systematic test viewpoints, oversights in detailed test viewpoints, and defect convergence. This is how oversights in testing are prevented. The perspectives used for exit criteria in software testing include a variety of different ideas other than quality accounting. The key is to apply exit criteria in software testing from a diverse range of perspectives. This leads to precise exit criteria in software testing. It is important to maintain diverse standards for exit criteria in software testing while implementing exit criteria in software testing.

[3] Short cycle management based on data

Problems can be grasped soon after they occur by implementing management based on data in short cycles that are at least weekly. Furthermore, in the case of face-to-face management, communication is improved, and it becomes easier to take actions with substance rather than just form. The results of the CMMI Level 5 organization survey (see section 2.6 in chapter 2) indicated the difficulty of achieving substantive results. For substantive results to be produced, management checks must not be overly focused on simple changes in numerical values or formal reports, but instead must grasp precisely what is actually occurring on-site.

In the example of Organization B (see section 7.3 in chapter 7), the revision of methods for holding project management meetings played an important role in improving quality. The management style of receiving reports after problems are solved only leads to the rubber-stamping of problem resolution results. By quickly understanding problems after they occur, and implementing countermeasures after precisely ascertaining the true cause of that problem while all concerned parties reach an agreement, and by concluding by verifying data for the actual state of affairs on-site, it becomes possible for the concerned parties to bring together and utilize the experience and know-how of each individual. This leads to the organized sharing and utilization of each individual's experience and know-how.

[4] Quality confirmation from both process and product angles using independent quality assurance departments

One of the representative examples of a case where a number of Japanese corporations have arrived at the same implementation method is the existence of a quality assurance department that is independent from the development department. Although the functions performed by the quality assurance department differ somewhat depending on the corporation, the method is the same. The state of process completion is grasped by analyzing data during development from an objective standpoint, while the quality of work output is verified for each process, and final work output is actually tested and evaluated. This type of quality assurance department is particular to the Japanese corporation, and similar examples are not seen elsewhere on the global level. By establishing a quality assurance department as a fixed organization, quality assurance know-how and examples are collected in one place, with the benefit that it is possible to apply feedback to the shared processes of the entire organization. A decision at the organization level is required to establish an independent quality assurance department.

Even if a development department is excellent, it is still difficult to constantly maintain an objective viewpoint throughout development. The tendency is to always think from a perspective that favors the developer's preferences. In order to successfully judge from the customer's perspective, it is necessary to have a function that can determine quality from an independent standpoint, without being influenced by the development department. Furthermore, it is also important to make decisions from both process quality and product quality angles. Process quality is assured by reliably executing everything that must be executed in each process, and product quality is assured by satisfying all the prescribed requirements in the completed work output. Process quality and product quality are in a mutually complementary relationship, so it is not possible to properly grasp quality from just one side. By adding the quality assurance that was missing from the product side, Organization B was able to place its overall improvements measures on track. The verification of quality from both process and product angles is a basic principle of quality management.

[5] Release decision-making by multiple people

The use of multiple people in release decision-making is another mechanism that is implemented in the same way by multiple Japanese corporations. When release decision-making is performed alone by the person in charge of the development project, because he is responsible for that project, he will tend to make decisions that are in the best interests of the developer. By having those outside the project's command structure also be involved in release decision-making, it becomes possible to conduct release decision-making from the customer's perspective. With this type of a system, inconvenient facts also form the basis of the decision, and this enables release decision-making that is fair. The person in charge of the quality assurance department is the best example of a decider from a different command structure.

Since multiple people are involved in release decision-making, it is necessary to plan in advance the method for deciding what to do if the determination result is split. It is not appropriate to leave the final determination up to the person in charge of the project, because the intention behind using multiple people in release decision-making is always to enable the use of release decision-making from the customer's perspective, not to make decisions based on the developer's preferences. The ideal final decider is the head of the quality assurance department. This implementation method is one that is shared by Japanese corporations. By leaving the final determination up to the head of the quality assurance department, the responsibility and authority for quality assurance from the customer's perspective is given to the quality assurance department. Due to this, a high degree of professionalism is expected of the quality assurance department, and this has a beneficial influence on the activities in "[4] quality confirmation from both process and product angles using independent quality assurance departments". A virtuous cycle is born whereby the awareness of professionalism increases in the quality assurance department, quality technology improves, and precise quality assurance is executed.

Furthermore, release decision-making standards should include the results of "[4] quality confirmation from both process and product angles using independent quality assurance departments" in addition to the results of "[2] implementation of testing with precise exit criteria in software testing". Release decision-making is the final barrier that prevents a software product with problems from being shipped to the customer. It is important for release decision-making standards to steadily apply feedback from examples of failed release decision-making in the past, and to use multiple redundant and diverse decision elements in order to improve the precision of the release decision.

9.5 Improvements in Human Components

As was made clear in the results of the CMMI Level 5 organization survey (see section 2.6 in chapter 2), member awareness and an organizational culture that emphasizes quality are indispensable for quality improvement. There is no conclusive technology for resolving how to improve human components, so there is no option other than to cultivating member awareness and organizational culture that emphasize quality in the execution of specific measures. The important part of improving human components is ensuring that the top level of an organization has a strong will to improve quality. Having the top of the organization continuously show the importance of quality improvement is the first step towards fostering a culture that emphasizes quality in that organization. Having multiple people participate in fair release decision-making also has a positive influence on cultivating an organizational culture that emphasizes quality. Reliably making decisions based on evaluation standards from the customer's perspective causes decision-making standards that never change to be born inside the organization. The organization's constituent members all think and make decisions from the customer's perspective. On the other hand, in the case of an organization where unchanging decision-making is not guaranteed, decision-making standards change based on the standpoint and the situation, and top management makes decisions based on how they are thinking at the time as well as each separate item, so the organization's members must await and adhere to the decisions of top management. Whether or not decisions are made based on unchanging evaluation standards has a decisive influence on that organization's respect for self-initiative.

As these eight success factors are implemented, changes should be seen in the actions taken by that organization's engineers. During Organization B's improvements as well (see section 7.3 in chapter 7), changes were seen in the behavior of the engineers, with the number of times the importance of quality was mentioned by engineers increasing in the approximately two-year period. Organization C (see section 7.4, chapter 7) showed a similar experience. There is no technique for directly improving human components. The continuous execution of these eight success factors, however, is the most reliable method of improving human components.

9.6 Considerations

The first consideration is the relationship between the overall picture of high-quality software development success factors and software quality accounting.

Of the high-quality software development success factors, the ones that can be achieved through software quality accounting are the project level management success factors "[1] early quality assurance through reviews" and "[2] implementation of testing with precise exit criteria in software testing". Success factors [3] to [5] are mechanisms that were invented to elicit the effects of software quality accounting, and have a high level of affinity with quality accounting. Therefore, project level management success factors can be achieved through the application of software quality accounting. Of course, this is not meant to deny the applicability of other techniques, and it is necessary to consider appropriate techniques based on the software attributes.

It goes without saying that the organization level management success factors "[1] setting quality improvement targets based on external benchmarks" and "[2] process improvement based on follow-up on quality improvement targets" should be achieved if a quality management system based on a standard such as ISO 9001 is implemented. The key point is the adoption of external benchmarks that reflect the customer's opinion for the software quality improvement targets. Also, "[3] provision of systems integrating software development methodologies, tools, and development environments" is an item that should be aggressively pursued as a software development organization. The systems described in success factor [3] are designed to thoroughly reduce the secondary difficulty of software. These systems represent the accumulated know-how and expertise of the site of development, and it is thought that the construction of effective systems requires a process of trial and error over a certain length of time.

The next consideration is the relationship between management at the project and organization levels. In order to ensure a project can succeed, management is implemented at the project level while maintaining a certain set of project conditions. In order to continuously improve the success rate of projects executed at a software development organization, however, it is mandatory to implement management at the organization level. The "kaizen" approach demanded by "[2] process improvement based on follow-up on quality improvement targets" is particularly important. "Kaizen" is not a simple one-time process revision, but rather a constant effort by all members of the organization from top to bottom to revise everyday processes while thinking of methods that might be better than the current methods. It is because the idea of "kaizen" is at the foundation that process improvement constantly progresses, and the systems of "[3] provision of systems integrating software development methodologies, tools, and development environments" are constantly revised to be the latest most easy-to-use systems. This has a positive influence on projects and increases the rate of success.

The final considerations are the overall picture of the high-quality software success factors presented in this chapter, the relationship with CMMI, and the meaning of what this chapter proposes.

CMMI defines 22 process areas, and the goal of each process area is achieved by the integrated implementation of all of the practices in that process area. Although the methods of implementation are left up to the user, and so there is a high level of flexibility, even at level 5 there is no guarantee that the standard for the post-release defect count will be high, as described in section 2.6. This is also demonstrated in the post-release defect count before Organization B's improvements. Although functional omissions and insufficiencies in the software process definitely tend to cause an increase in the post-release defect count, this does not mean that all 22 process areas are mandatory. Organization A, which invented quality accounting, succeeded in reducing its post-release defect count to 1/20th of the previous count before CMMI was even invented, and its construction of quality accounting did not cover all 22 process areas.

Based on all this, it is thought that the construction of systems for high-quality software development does not need to cover all 22 of the process areas proposed by CMMI. In fact, it may be more efficient to construct the necessary processes by using methods that set quality improvement targets by reflecting the opinions of customers, and that can grasp and resolve the omissions and insufficiencies in the processes necessary for that organization. This is achieved through the success factors [1] to [3] that are proposed as a means of management from the organization's perspective. The customer's opinions are incorporated through "[1] setting quality improvement targets based on external benchmarks", and processes are improved by reflecting a customer orientation through "[2] process improvement based on follow-up on quality improvement targets". The results are reflected in "[3] provision of systems integrating software development methodologies, tools, and development environments", and these systems are provided to the engineers.

Furthermore, it is important to emphasize the point that as a result of the software quality improvement efforts carried out in the 1970s by NEC and a number of other Japanese corporations, the same implementation methods were arrived at, and these shared practices should be aggressively implemented. The effectiveness of these practices has been verified by multiple corporations. The success factors [1] through [5] that are included in project level management are these shared practices. Each of these practices should be effective if the goals are understood in their execution.

9.7　Conclusion

This chapter discussed the success factors and the overall picture of high-quality software development.

The success factors of high-quality software development were derived by combining the practices demonstrated by a number of Japanese corporations with the author's more than 20 years of experience and research at NEC. These factors are characterized by the fact that they incorporate evaluations from the customer's perspective as quality improvement targets while also combining the practices that have already been demonstrated by multiple corporations in their construction.

When one considers all eight of these success factors together, it becomes apparent that they all show a customer orientation. Thinking of the best ways to bring the customer's perspective into the process of software development while successfully developing software is the key to high-quality software development.

Chapter 10.   Summary and Final Conclusions

The introduction introduced the problem of the second "Software Crisis". This dissertation proposes one strategy for overcoming this crisis.

This dissertation adheres to an approach of emphasizing techniques that have actually been demonstrated. The effectiveness of every technique presented in this dissertation has been verified by multiple organizations. The combination of demonstrated techniques makes the achievement of high-quality software development possible.

Chapter 2 defined the meanings of the terms "quality" and "defect". This dissertation defines "quality" as the "degree to which a set of inherent characteristics fulfills requirements", and indicates that quality is determined by the standards of customers who receive those requirements. The definition of "defect" is somewhat wider than the usual scope of the term, and includes attributes that should exist within the scope. In other words, the defects as referred to within this dissertation include not only the narrow sense of reliability, but rather the overall attributes that the customer expects to exist as well. Furthermore, not only is it important to manage quality assurance from both process and product angles, quality management also includes the two perspectives of organization and project. In the discussion of software attributes, it was explained that the difficulties of software development include both the inherent difficulty of building and demonstrating the correctness of concepts, and the secondary difficulties surrounding the process of implementing software in terms of the necessary meticulousness and accuracy. This secondary difficulty can be resolved, and by thoroughly resolving it, the inherent difficulty can also be somewhat ameliorated. In addition, based on the results of a survey conducted regarding organizations that are at Level 5 in CMMI, which is the de facto standard of software process improvement, the factors influencing quality improvement and the effects of CMMI were discussed. The results of the CMMI Level 5 organization survey were used in order to analyze the factors affecting quality improvement, based on the condition that there are no functional flaws in processes. As a result, it was shown that it is difficult to achieve quality with CMMI of a high enough level such that the low post-release defect count can be used as a strength. For high-quality software development to be achieved, it is necessary to construct processes that can have substantive effects while improving human components as well.

167

Chapter 3 provided an overview and a description of the application method of software quality accounting, which was invented on the site of software development at NEC, and which was constructed and applied over the course of more than 20 years. The major characteristics of software quality accounting are early quality assurance based on the detection of defects through reviews, and precise exit criteria in software testing. These two characteristics greatly contribute to the realization of high-quality software development. Chapter 4 described the "defect root cause analysis and 1+n procedure" software quality accounting technique in detail, while clarifying the differences between this technique and "five whys analysis". Although defect root cause analysis is often used at sites of software development, it is also a technique that is difficult to use effectively. The reason for this is that it does not analyze based on an awareness of the structure of root causes, and the resolution of this problem would be difficult with the general-purpose five whys analysis. In addition, the "defect root cause analysis and 1+n procedure" technique is used to analyze root causes with an awareness of the structure of root causes, and so it is a technique optimized for use in same-type defect detection.

Chapter 5 discussed the techniques used to support software quality accounting, including review technologies and the mechanisms for quality assurance surrounding quality accounting. The three mechanisms for quality assurance include short-cycle management based on data, quality confirmation by an independent quality assurance department from both process and product angles, and release decision-making by multiple people. These three mechanisms were also implemented by a number of other Japanese corporations as a part of software quality improvement efforts starting in the 1970s, and as a result, they are shared by multiple corporations. The fact that these mechanisms have been demonstrated by not just one corporation but rather multiple corporations is key.

Chapter 6 introduced the "Software Factory", which is a system integrating software development methodologies, tools, and development environments. The Software Factory is an important measure for resolving the difficulties surrounding the process of implementation, including the meticulousness and accuracy of development work and work output as required by software development. It is because of the provision of the development foundation that is the Software Factory that engineers are freed from the requirement to provide software with the attributes of accuracy and meticulousness that do not allow for even one character being mistaken, so that they can focus on the intrinsic difficulty of the software itself, which is inventing concepts and validating their correctness.

Chapter 7 discussed the actual examples of software quality accounting application by Organizations A , B and C. Organization A is the organization that invented software quality accounting, and while constructing this technique, it reduced post-release defect counts to 1/20th of their previous levels, and maintained the new low levels for more than 20 years since. Organization B is an organization that suffered from high post-release defect counts in spite of the fact that it had achieved CMMI Level 5. This organization also succeeded in lowering its post-release defect counts by strictly applying the software quality accounting technique, and by upgrading the mechanisms surrounding quality accounting. Organization B set as its target the achievement of post-release defect counts at the same level as at Organization A, and now that four years have gone by, it is showing smooth progress towards that target and is expected to achieve it in the remaining year. The example of Organization C describes the quality improvements of an offshore development organization in China. Based on a step-up model invented for use by offshore development organizations, not only did it strictly apply quality accounting, it also upgraded the mechanisms surrounding quality accounting. Based on this, Organization C was able to achieve improvements in the quality of the developed products it delivers to its client organization, improvements in productivity (line/person-hour [H]), improvements in Japanese language abilities, and a reductions in development costs. It is highly significant that this organization was able to demonstrate that by strengthening reviews, it was able to successfully reduce regression work while lowering the overall cost of development. This chapter demonstrated not only that post-release defect counts can be lowered and maintained by applying software quality accounting and upgrading the surrounding mechanisms, it also showed that this method is effective for offshore development organizations as well. The most important point to emphasize here is that it is necessary to upgrade the surrounding mechanisms while at the same time applying software quality accounting.

Chapter 8 discussed the engineering values of the software quality accounting technique, which were touched upon in chapter 7 as well. The five engineering values of quality accounting are early quality assurance through reviews, precise exit criteria in software testing, improvement in issue resolution capabilities through defect root cause analysis, value as a driver of quality improvements, and emphasizing a hands-on approach. Since there are not many techniques available that provide the same values as any of these items, this increases the importance of quality accounting techniques.

Chapter 9 discussed the overall picture of high-quality software development success factors, based on the chapters up to chapter 8. The success factors behind high-quality software development include the three organization level management factors, or [1] setting quality improvement targets based on external benchmarks, [2] process improvement based on follow-up on quality improvement targets, and [3] provision of systems integrating software development methodologies, tools, and development environments, and the five project level management factors, or [1] early quality assurance through reviews, [2] implementation of testing with precise exit criteria in software testing, [3] short cycle management based on data, [4] quality confirmation from both process and product angles using independent quality assurance departments, and [5] release decision-making by multiple people. Of the project level management factors, [1] and [2] can be achieved through software quality accounting. The remaining factors [3] through [5] correspond to the mechanisms surrounding quality accounting. Implementing the five project level management factors, makes it possible for the implemented project to be successful. The three organization level management factors increase the success rate of projects implemented by that organization. The construction of effective processes and the improvement of human components by implementing these eight success factors make it possible to repeatedly decide fairly from the customer's perspective, which never changes.

Looking forward, there are two issues that will affect the future of high-quality software development.

The first issue is the modeling that will enable the practical application of the overall picture of the success factors of high-quality software development. This dissertation described the success factors of high-quality software development and an overall picture of these success factors. In order to enable the application of these success factors at an actual site of software development, it will be necessary to break them down into their component parts and assign priority rankings, in order to clarify the sequence of application on-site, while modeling in such a way as to explain the details of each component. For instance, in order to achieve the project level management factor "[3] short cycle management based on data", it will be necessary to organize and prioritize application items, including the clarification of data items to collect, data analysis methods, and the crystallization of items that must be discussed from a management angle. This also goes for the relationships between success factors. It will also be necessary to clarify a standard that can clearly explain each success factor's goals while enabling the determination of process effectiveness levels. This will make it possible for any software development organization to apply this model. Furthermore, the model must be actually applied in a trial run, and feedback of the results of this trial run will also be required. This will streamline the steps that should be taken by any corporation pursuing the implementation of high-quality software development.

Once it is in a form whereby it can be actually applied, the second issue is the application of a model of the overall picture of the success factors of high-quality software development to the actual site of software development, and an analysis of the results. As has been indicated for a long time, the quality and productivity of developed software are greatly influenced by the developer's technology level as well as by the excellence of the software processes. This fact will be demonstrated using actual development data in order to back up the validity of the model of the overall picture of success factors behind high-quality software development, while at the same time acting as material to be used for the widespread enlightenment of society. In order to overcome the second "Software Crisis", society must recognize the attributes and difficulties of software, as well as the conditions of high-quality software development.

This dissertation shows a method for grappling with the attributes of software, which is something humanity has not encountered before the present era, by combining knowledge with techniques that have been constructed based on a foundation of many years of on-site effort, and by demonstrating the same. It would be fortunate if this dissertation could contribute in some way to the advancement of the software industry.

References

[1-1] T. Tamai, *Destination of the Software society*, Iwanami shyoten, Tokyo, 2012.

[1-2] CMU Software Engineering Institute, *CMMI for Development, Version 1.3(CMMI-DEV, V1.3)*, CMU/SEI-2010-TR-033, 2010.

[2-1] ISO9000:2005, *Quality Management Systems –Fundamentals and Vocabulary*

[2-2] R. S. Pressman, *Software engineering -a practitioner's approach-*, McGraw-Hill Science, New York, 2004.

[2-3] G. M. Weinberg, *Quality Software Management Vol. 1: Systems Thinking*, Dorset House Publishing, NewYork, 1992.

[2-4] J. Martin, *Rapid Application Development*, Macmillan Coll Div, 1991.

[2-5] K. Ishikawa, *Japanese-style Quality Management - What is TQC? -* , JUSE press, 1981.

[2-6] N. Kano, N. Serak, F. Takahashi and S. Tsuji, *Attractive quality and mast-be quality*, Journal "Hinshitsu" of the Japanese Society for Quality Control (JSQC), Vol.14,No.2, pp.39-48,1984.

[2-7] Y. Iizuka, *Modern Quality Management*, Asakura Publishing Co., Ltd., Tokyo, 2009.

[2-8] ISO/IEC 9126-1:2001, *Information Technology - Software Product Quality - Part 1 : Quality Model*

[2-9] ISO/IEC 2382-14:1997. *Information technology - Vocabulary- Reliability, maintainability, and availability*

[2-10] M. V. Mäntylä and C. Lassenius, What Types of Defects Are Really Discovered in Code Reviews?, IEEE Transactions on Software Engineering, Vol.35, No.3, pp.430-448,2009.

[2-11] W. S. Humphrey, *Introduction to the Personal Software Process*, Addison-Wesley Professional, New York, 1996.

[2-12] SQuBOK study team, *SQuBOK Guide - Software Quality Body of Knowledge -*, Ohmsya, Tokyo, 1997.

[2-13] Project Management Institute, *A Guide to the Project Management Body of Knowledge: (PMBOK Guide)*, Project Management Institute, 2008.

[2-14] F. P. Brooks Jr., *The Mythical Man-Month : Essays on Software Engineering, Anniversary Edition*, Addison-Wesley Professional, New York, 1995.

[2-15] N. Honda, Y. Nishi, Y. Katayama, H. Yagi, M. Takahashi and T. Chujo, *Study of*

Engineer's Motivation, Journal of the Society of Project Management, Vol.3,No.3,pp. 33-39,2001.

[2-16] M. Cusumano et al., *Software Development Worldwide: The State of the Practice*, *IEEE Software*, Vol.20, No.6, pp.34-38, 2003.

[3-1] JUSE SPC Study Team, *Software Quality Assurance Technologies toward Twenty First century*, JUSE Press, Tokyo, 1994.

[3-2] H. Kubo, *Software Quality Assurance at Fujitsu*, JUSE Press, Tokyo, 1989.

[3-3] K.Yasuda, *Software Quality Assurance Methodology and Practice*, JUSE Press, Tokyo, 1995.

[3-4] T.Okazaki, *Software Testing and Quality Assurance*, J-TECHNO, Tokyo, 1999.

[3-5] M. A. Cusumano, *Japan's Software Factories*, Oxford University Press, New York, 1991.

[3-6] Y.Mizuno, *Software Total Quality Control*, JUSE Press, Tokyo, 1991.

[3-7] N. Honda and T. Mano, *How to estimate for software development*, JUSE Press, Tokyo, 1993.

[3-8] N. Honda, R. Kurashita, and N. Tsuboi, *A Software Development Management System with a Template*, Proceedings of the India - Japan Conference on Quality in Software Systems Engineering, pp.2-14, 1997.

[3-9] N. Honda, *Software Quality Accounting System - Quality assurance technology that supports high quality software development at NEC -*, JUSE Press, Tokyo, 2010.

[3-10] B. W. Boehm and R. Turner, *Balancing Agility and Discipline: A Guide for the Perplexed*, Addison-Wesley Professional, New York, 2003.

[3-11] B. W. Boehm, *Software Engineering Economics*, Prentice-Hall, Englewood Cliffs, NJ, 1981.

[3-12] S. Yamada, *Elements of Software Reliability: Modeling Approach*, Kyoritsu Shuppan Co., Ltd., Tokyo, 2010.

[4-1] T. Ohno, *Toyota production system*, Diamond-press, Tokyo, 1978.

[4-2] Y. Iizuka and R. Kaneko, *Cause analysis and Architecture Model based Analysis*, JUSE Press, Tokyo, 2012.

[5-1] T. Gilb, and D. Graham, *Software Inspection*, Addison-Wesley Professional, New York, 1993.

[5-2] K. E. Wiegers, *Peer Reviews in Software: A Practical Guide*, Addison-Wesley Professional, New York, 2001.

[5-3] K. Ohnishi et al., *JSTQB certified Testing Engineer*, SHOEISYA, Tokyo, 2007.

[5-4] M. Nonaka, *Effect and Efficiency of Software Inspection*, the Journal of Information Processing Society of Japan, Vol.50, No.5, pp.385-390, 2009.

[5-5] Software Production Control (SPC) internationalization Taskforce, *Features of Software Quality Control in Japan and its Background*, Proceedings of the 22th SPC Symposium, pp.427-450, 2003.

[7-1] S. Sasabe and R. Kaneko, *Integrated Software Quality Management Based on Multiple Process Improvement Models and Organization's Own TQM Method – A new Process Network Oriented Method*, Proceedings of the 3rd World Congress for Software Quality, Vol.1, pp. 279-289, 2005.

[7-2] S-open Offshore development study team, *Software development Offshoring Perfect Guide*, NIKKEI BP, Tokyo, 2004.

[7-3] N. Honda, M. Noda, K. Kurata, N. Iizumi, K. Ohnishi, K. Sakuragi andF.Hotta, *Research and Analysis of Project Management for Offshore Software Development*, Proceedings of the Society of Project Management in 2004, pp. 377-382, 2004.

[7-4] N. Honda, M. Noda, K. Kurata, N. Iizumi, K. Ohnishi, K. Sakuragi andF.Hotta, *Case Study of Project Management improvement for Offshore Software Development*, Proceedings of the Society of Project Management in 2004, pp. 371-376, 2004.

[7-5] N. Honda and M. Matsumoto, *Quality and Productivity Improvement Model for Software Development*, Technical report of The Institute of Electronics, Information and Communication Enginerrs, Vol.105, No.255, pp. 7-12, 2005.

Study results

Research Papers

1. N. Honda, *Beyond CMMI Level 5 - Comparative Analysis of Two CMMI Level 5 Organizations* -, Software Quality Professional, Vol. 11, No.4,pp. 4-12, September 2009.

2. N. Honda and S. Yamada, *Characteristic Analysis of Software Development Organizations Having Great Success*, Proceedings of the 17th International Conference on Reliability and Quality in Design, pp.379-383, August 2011.

3. R. Kurashita, H. Yosimura, M. Nonaka and N. Honda, *Quantitative Evaluation of Software Design Quality by using CK Metrics Distributions*, Proceedings of the 31th SQiP 2011,CD-R,8 pp.,September 2011.

4. N. Koketsu, N. Honda, S. Kawamura, J. Nomura, and M. Nonaka, *Improvement of the Fault-prone Class Prediction by the Process Metrics Use*, Proceedings of the 5th World Congress for Software Quality (5WCSQ), CD-R,9 pp., November 2011.

5. T. Mori, R. Kurashita, and N. Honda, *Proposal of "Ask Why" Framework to Analyze Defect Root Causes*, Proceedings of the 5th World Congress for Software Quality (5WCSQ), CD-R,8 pp., November 2011.

6. N. Honda and S. Yamada, *Empirical Analysis for High Quality Software Development*, American Journal of Operations Research, Vol. 2, No.1, pp. 34-42, March 2012.

7. N. Honda and S. Yamada, *Defect Root-Cause Analysis and 1+n Procedure Technique to Improve Software Quality*, International Journal of Systems Assurance Engineering and Management, Vol. 3, No.2, pp.111-121, August 2012.

8. N. Honda and S. Yamada, *Software Quality and Productivity Improvement Activities at NEC*, Proceedings of the 11th International Conference of Industrial Management (ICIM2012), pp. 34-42, August 2012.

9. N. Honda and S. Yamada, *Success Factors to Achieve Excellent Quality - CMMI Level 5 Organizations Research Report* -, Software Quality Professional, Vol.14, No.4, pp.21-32, September 2012.

10. N. Honda and S. Yamada, *Realization of High Software Quality development by Applying Software Quality Accounting*, the Journal "Computer Software" of Japan Society for Software science and Technology, Vol. 30,No.2, pp.66-82,May 2013.

Related Research Papers

1. N. Honda, *Design Review for Software Development*, The Journal "Quality Management" of JUSE, Vol.60, No.8, pp. 34-41, August 2009.

2. N. Honda and S. Yamada, *Improvement of Software Quality during Review -Study of Software Quality Accounting (1)-*, Proceedings of the Society of Project Management in 2011, pp. 213-218, 2011.

3. N. Honda and S. Yamada, *Defect Root-Cause Analysis and 1+n Procedure technique - Study of Software Quality Accounting (2)-*, Proceedings of the Society of Project Management in 2011, pp. 157-162, 2011.

4. N. Honda and S. Yamada, *Software Quality Accounting - For High Quality Software Development -*, Journal of the Society of Project Management, Vol.13,No. 5,pp. 9-14,October 2011.

5. N. Honda, *Success Factors to Achieve Excellent Quality - CMMI Level 5 Organizations Research Report -*, Proceedings of the 4th Japan-Korea Software Management Symposium —Recent Development and Future Trend -, pp. 11-23, November 2011.

6. N. Honda, *High Quality Software Development beyond CMMI level 5,* Journal "Hinshitsu" of the Japanese Society for Quality Control (JSQC), Vol.42, No.4, pp.54-62, October 2012.

www.ingramcontent.com/pod-product-compliance
Lightning Source LLC
LaVergne TN
LVHW042335060326
832902LV00006B/181